James L. Ford

**Dolly Dillenbeck**

A portrayal of certain phases of metropolitanlife and character

James L. Ford

**Dolly Dillenbeck**
*A portrayal of certain phases of metropolitanlife and character*

ISBN/EAN: 9783743337503

Manufactured in Europe, USA, Canada, Australia, Japa

Cover: Foto ©ninafisch / pixelio.de

Manufactured and distributed by brebook publishing software (www.brebook.com)

James L. Ford

**Dolly Dillenbeck**

"SHE WAS A STRANGER IN THE TOWN."

Copyright, 1895, by
GEORGE H. RICHMOND & CO.

# DOLLY DILLENBECK

A PORTRAYAL OF CERTAIN PHASES OF
METROPOLITAN LIFE AND CHARACTER

BY

## JAMES L. FORD

AUTHOR OF "THE LITERARY SHOP," "HYPNOTIC TALES"
ETC., ETC.

ILLUSTRATED BY FRANCIS DAY

NEW-YORK
GEORGE H. RICHMOND & CO.
1895

# ILLUSTRATIONS

|  | PAGE |
|---|---|
| "She was a stranger in the town" *Frontispiece* | |
| "To the success of a certain young lady" | 64 |
| "The wine came, and close behind it lumbered Judge Doonothing" | 130 |
| "I don't care a snap of my finger for Mr. Hustle" | 196 |
| "The pop of the cork awoke Mr. Rungdown" | 260 |
| "A remarkably nice looking young woman" | 320 |

# DOLLY DILLENBECK

## CHAPTER I

At precisely two o'clock in the afternoon of a golden October day a young girl, slender, graceful, blonde, blue-eyed, and alone, passed through the wide doorway of the Grand Central Depot and stood for a brief moment on the sidewalk, a somewhat noticeable figure in the passing throng.

That she was a stranger in the town was made apparent by her clothes, which were unmistakably of provincial cut; and it seemed to the passers-by who glanced at her that her face, which, by the way, was perfectly calm and composed, ought to have worn the timid, shrinking, half-frightened look which is associated in the mind of every story-reader and play-goer with that most interesting and promising of all romantic characters, the village maiden alone in the great city. Standing in front of the depot in the full glare of the bright autumn sun, she might easily have passed herself off as the heroine of a weekly story-paper serial or of a melodrama of metropolitan life. And curiously enough, just as she emerged from the depot she stepped, unknowingly, into the pages of this story; for it was at that very moment that a well-dressed young man of about three and twenty came suddenly upon the scene—having been evolved somehow from the vast wilderness of tall houses—and beheld for the first time the slender, blue-eyed girl who was looking about her at the great, smoky, bustling, crowded city which was to be her home.

If the young girl had been a diligent student of the drama she would have recognized in the newcomer the stage hero of the commonly accepted type; for he carried himself with an air of self-possession and complacency thoroughly in keeping with his attire, which was, to say the least, quite abreast of the latest and most pronounced styles. His features were regular, and their expression good-natured. There were lines about his mouth and chin which indicated weakness of character and irresolution, and seemed somehow to be in complete accord with the silk waistcoat, the gaudy cravat, and the rings and other bits of finery which decked his person.

A stout, rather pompous-looking gentleman with a distinctively military air accompanied our *jeune premier*, and both stopped in their walk to survey the village maiden, who was standing with her satchel in her hand looking up at the elevated railroad and listening to the ceaseless roar of the city.

"By Jove!" cried the younger of the two men; "there's a deuced pretty girl. Looks like a simple village maiden, I should say. Probably she's just got in from the country somewhere. Upon my soul, I'd like to make her acquaintance. I wonder where she's going to, General? Don't you think we could find out?"

"She *is* a pretty girl," responded his companion; "and I should judge from the cut of her garments that she has just escaped from the parental nest somewhere among the hilltops. But look here, Dolly, my boy, it seems to me that you've got your hands full just now. Don't start in to make that poor young girl miserable before she's been half an hour in the town." And the General administered a sly nudge to his companion, who was now grinning in an engaging manner in the hope of rendering the young woman an instant prey to his charms.

"There she goes," said the younger of the two, rather ruefully, as the country maiden stepped into a Fourth Avenue car and disappeared from his sight. But the grin broke out afresh on his simple face as he saw her turn her head and cast one glance in his direction just as she gained the car platform.

"Caught on, by Jove!" he cried excitedly. "Let 's call a cab and follow her!"

But the General had reached that time of life when rapid journeys in cabs, and other adventurous phases of metropolitan life, had become distasteful to him; and besides, he had not had a drink since noon, and he was getting very hungry into the bargain. That made three reasons for not going in pursuit of the car, whereas the young man could offer but one in favor of it.

The three reasons, combined with the General's superior weight and age, resulted in their adjourning immediately for luncheon, the younger man accepting the other's comforting assurance that he would be sure to run across her before long, and it would be a great deal better not to run after her, but rather to let her seek him out.

That night Dolly Dillenbeck sat at a round table in a café on upper Broadway with his friend and mentor General Whiffletree. For some moments the pair had been sitting silently smoking and sipping green mint, when Dolly suddenly broke out:

"I tell you what it is, General, it seems to me that there's a screw loose somewhere in this world of ours."

"How do you mean?" asked the old warrior, with assumed interest.

"I mean this way," rejoined the other. "When a young girl comes into this town a stranger, alone and unsophisticated, the odds are dead against her. It's too bad; but anyway, I stand ready to do what's right by her, provided—"

"Right by whom?" demanded the General, suddenly sitting bolt upright and manifesting a decided interest in what Dolly was saying.

"Why, that girl we saw this afternoon. I've been thinking of her ever since, and I'm going to get acquainted with her somehow. But, by Jove! I sort of hate to do it. I know what the result 'll be — young, green country girl meeting a man of the world, an — well — an experienced man like myself, for the first time. However, I'm afraid she's a goner; for really, she's too pretty a piece of goods to be neglected." And Dolly settled his high collar with a complacent leer, while the General finished his noisy arctic explorations among the chopped ice in his glass and wagged his head jocosely.

"Ah, my boy," he said, "I'm afraid you're going to make sad havoc here in this town before you finish your career. Better be careful, though."

"But after all, old man," continued the other, "what a shame it is that society is so constituted as to make the woman the sufferer, and yet condone the fault of the man, who in the sight of Heaven is surely just as much to blame as she is—if not more so! Did you ever think of that?"

"Yes," said the General dryly; "I've noticed that one of the two generally gets it in the neck."

## CHAPTER II

AT the period of which I write, Dolly Dillenbeck had been scarcely a twelvemonth "on the turf," if I may quote one of his own pet phrases, while the young girl who is to play the opposite part to him in the pages to follow had spent less than one week of her whole life in the city of New York, and presumably knew very little of the dangers which beset the innocent and simple-minded ones who attempt to swim in the metropolitan current. Dolly, however, was town-bred, and had been carefully reared in the solitude of a great brown-stone house situated in those famous preserves of wealth and respectability which cluster about Madison Avenue.

His father, Jacob Dillenbeck, had, in the course of a half-century of toil, parsimony, and narrow thinking and living, amassed a fortune, of which the brownstone house was a symbol; and his only son had received during his boyhood the most careful training that his hard-headed father and his seriously minded mother could bestow upon him.

The Dillenbecks, father and mother, had come to New York some time in the early forties from the small Pennsylvania town in which both had been born and reared. Jacob had found employment in the store of an old Quaker merchant whose thrift and caution were proverbial in mercantile circles; and it was in the household of his employer that Sophia Lutz, his former playmate, was installed a year later as maid-of-all-work. Here Jacob pursued, with characteristic caution and leisure, the courtship which he had begun years before in the hay-field beside her father's house; and soon after the close of the first half of the century they were married and set up housekeeping in what was then Greenwich Village, where they resided until the close of the war, when they purchased, with a small portion of the wealth acquired during the exciting period of the contest, the brownstone house that stood in what is to-day one of the very best residential quarters of the town.

It was in this house that Dolly, their only child, was born the year after their removal from the old house in the old-fashioned and democratic quarter on the west side of the town; and the wife gave devout thanks to the God who had at last answered her prayers, and vowed that she would consecrate her son to a life-work that should be higher and nobler than the sordid money-grubbing to which her husband had given the full strength of his manhood, and which—such is the force of habit — engrossed all the thought and vigor of his riper years.

Long before she had weaned her boy the mother had determined in her own mind exactly how he should be brought up, and what his course should be when he attained to years of discretion. Henceforth she would have but one duty in life — to fit him for the part he was to play in the world, to guard him from all contact with evil.

The Dillenbecks took no part in the social life of the town. Their minds were cast in too serious a mold to permit a taste on the part of either for the frivolities which claimed so much of the time and attention of their worldly minded neighbors. Mrs. Dillenbeck had a few friends of her own sex and her own way of thinking. As they usually agreed with her on all subjects, she had great confidence in their judgment, and it was to them that she confided her plans for the careful bringing up of her son.

They listened attentively, and subsequently agreed without a dissenting voice that little Adolphus was in a fair way to become a model of his sex. If wine and spirits were denied him in his youth he would be sure to abhor them when he reached manhood. If he were brought up in utter ignorance of the allurements which Satan offers to the young in the shape of theaters, balls, billiards, gaming, and other iniquitous works, the playhouse, the ball-room, and the dice-box would have no charm for him. There was no need of his going into business or adopting a profession. Thanks to his father's half-century of toil, the son would inherit a fortune large enough to enable him to live without working, and so keep himself unspotted of the world. That was what the devout woman dreaded more than anything else — the contamination of worldly minded and evil associates.

Quietly the years rolled by in the big

brown house. Nurses, governesses, and tutors came and went until Dolly reached the age of thirteen, when it had been decided six years before that he was to be sent to school. Mrs. Dillenbeck herself took him to Dr. Euclid's small and exceedingly exclusive academy for the training of the young, and left him clinging to his desk and looking with frightened eyes at the youngsters about him, who were grinning in anticipation of the fun they would have with him at recess. That hour of recreation had scarcely begun when the new boy's howls brought the Doctor on a quick run to the back yard, which served as a playground; and poor Dolly was dragged from the midst of a circle of active young lads who had opened a fusillade on him with their pea-shooters and were dancing about him in imitation of Indian warriors torturing a captive.

"What right have you to pitch upon young Dillenbeck?" demanded the principal, with as much severity as he dared assume toward pupils who were worth a hundred dollars apiece to him every six months in the year.

"What right has he to wear long curls like a girl?" retorted an exclusive young gentleman who was accustomed to hear his father grumble about the Doctor's charges and intimate that he regarded the reverend instructor as little better than a humbug.

To the school-boy mind this reply seemed to be freighted with unanswerable logic; and from that moment until the end of the week, when Dolly's school-days ended forever, he was regarded, even by the most sedate and decorous of Dr. Euclid's pupils, as a legitimate butt for every bit of practical humor that intelligent and rebellious youngsters are capable of perpetrating.

For a few days the unhappy boy endured the buffetings of his tormentors with a dumb meekness that was akin to courage, and that in the end might have won for him the tolerance and then the regard of his mates if it had not been that the story of his tribulations, concerning which the child had breathed not a single word at home, reached his mother's ears in some roundabout way and caused her to write an indignant letter to the Doctor, calling him to account because of what she called his inhuman treatment of her only son, who, she assured him, should never cross his threshold again.

That Dolly's unhappiness was the direct and legitimate result of her own unreasoning folly in rearing him as if he had been a delicate girl instead of the fairly robust boy that he was, never entered Mrs. Dillenbeck's narrow mind. On the contrary, she became more confident than she ever had been before that the young could not be too carefully guarded from the world, and she resolved that his education should be continued at home under restrictions even more severe than those which she had originally intended.

It was an awful mistake to send him to school at all. If it had not been for his father's persistence she never would have agreed to it. Her son was not fitted to associate with the evil-minded little ruffians who, she was sure, had deliberately intended to kill him, and from whose clutches he had fortunately been rescued. She shuddered as she thought of the possible results of constant companionship with those little wretches.

And so the old tutor was recalled, and in the stillness of the great house Adolphus Dillenbeck listlessly acquired an almost useless education. The precise old pedagogue who taught him—Mrs. Dillenbeck had no faith in young men, who were sure to be worldly minded and full of modern irreverence—had no thought of anything that was not contained within the covers of the dry text-books with which the boy worked; and long before his period of tutelage was ended, books had become to him nothing less than an abhorrence. All novels and story-books, which might have interested him in something and quickened his imagination, were carefully kept from him, because, as his mother remarked, they "led down to death and destruction"; and for other equally logical reasons he was never taken to any of the places of interest in or near the city, or taught that there was any real connection between his dreary lesson-books and the world in which he lived.

So it happened that so long as his parents lived Dolly was kept in a dull, narrow path, on either side of which the dreary hedges of needless and exasperating precaution rose high above his head, shutting him out from nearly all the cheering, healthful sunshine of life that is the rightful heritage of youth.

One evening, soon after he had entered upon his seventeenth year, he went with his parents to pay a visit to some friends who lived in a remote quarter of the town; and as the carriage rolled along upper Broadway, Dolly looked out in wonder at the gay, brilliantly lighted street, through which crowds of well-dressed, happy-looking people were hurrying to places of amusement or strolling in idle ease. He saw the wide-open door of a famous playhouse, with a long line of men crowding up to the box-office; he noticed the groups that stood about the doorways of the hotels and cafés, and the stragglers who paused to inspect the beautiful things in the show-windows, or to enter the stores to make purchases for Christmas, which was close at hand. And just as the carriage turned into a side street, Dolly's glance fell upon a couple who were seated by the corner window of a fashionable restaurant. The man was young and well dressed, and appeared to be on thoroughly good terms with himself as well as with his companion, who seemed to the dazzled young Dillenbeck to be the most brilliantly beautiful and stunning young woman that his eyes had ever rested upon. She wore a large hat with an ostrich plume in it, and her face was sparkling with animation as she leaned across the table and talked to the young man opposite her. There was a smile on his face as he listened, and Dolly noticed that he held in his hand a bottle, and was carefully filling with some bright, sparkling fluid the tall glass that stood at the young girl's plate.

That one glimpse of Broadway made a deeper impression on the boy's brain than anything that had come into his life since the single week of unhappiness that constituted his school-days. He remembered it as a confused vision of shop-windows, electric lights, and people; but the couple in the restaurant window, the young man pouring the wine into the glass of the superb creature with the big ostrich plume waving above her laughing face, formed a picture that remained in his memory for many a long day—a picture in which not a single line or dot was confused or blurred.

From some remote, easy-going Dutch ancestor there had come down to this boy through generations of thrifty, hardheaded forebears a taste for the pleasures of life which he had never had an opportunity to gratify; and young as he was, his soul longed for those bright, intoxicating phases of existence of which he had obtained a single fleeting glimpse through the plate-glass window of his mother's carriage as it whirled swiftly through the brightly lighted streets. He used to lie awake at night and think of the couple in the restaurant window, resolving that in the years to come he would sit there too, and fill high the glass of a beautiful woman, whose laughing face would look up at his from beneath the shade of a big hat with a nodding, waving plume.

In his dreams he saw no other face but hers. Her companion was always himself, grown to manhood and richly clothed, pouring a foaming draft into the tall wine-glass, with the whole world looking in upon him through the great sheets of plate-glass, envying him his good fortune, agape at his audacity.

Dolly had not reached his majority when his mother died, devoutly thankful that she had been able to keep her boy from wine-bibbing, novel-reading, theater-going, and all the other worldly amusements which lead down to death and destruction; and a few months later old Jacob Dillenbeck went the way of all flesh, cheered by the thought of the bank-account and rent-roll which were a living, tangible proof that he had not allowed the single talent intrusted to him to rust in a napkin.

When the affairs of the dead merchant were settled, Dolly, the sole heir, found himself the possessor of a fortune of more than half a million dollars, all admirably well invested. As he had never before had a dollar that he had not been compelled to account for, he had extremely vague notions of the purchasing power of such a large sum, although he was morally sure that it was sufficient to maintain him in luxury for the rest of his life.

It was at Cold Brook Farm that his father died; and acting on the advice of the executors of the estate, Dolly remained in the country until late in the fall; for he decided at once to rent the big brownstone house in New York, and secure lodgings for himself in some more lively and agreeable part of the city. Life, with all its glorious possibilities of adventure and enjoyment, was opening before him; and it seemed to him that the bright lights of Broadway which still shone in his memory burned all the more brightly because he was so soon to join the throng that dwelt within their rays.

He wondered, as he walked or drove along the shady country roads, whether the couple that he had seen in the restaurant window were still to be found there feasting and drinking and making merry. Perhaps he would be able to make the acquaintance of that showy young creature, who was in all probability an actress, or something equally fascinating.

There were the theaters, too. He had never seen the inside of one in his life; but he had seen posters on the fences and in show-windows which had conveyed to his mind certain inflamed ideas of the attractions which they had to offer. He would go to a play the very night of his arrival in the city, and that would be within a few short days.

Above all, he determined that his life should be spent not in the quiet of a respectable side street, but in the very midst of the gay life for which his soul yearned.

# CHAPTER III

So it happened that Dolly turned up one bright afternoon on upper Broadway, walked into a large and gaudy hotel, and inscribed the name "T. Adolphus Dillenbeck" on the register with an air that gave the quick-witted room-clerk a fairly correct idea as to what manner of man he was. Having become a guest of the house, Dolly's first act was to ring his bell and order a bottle of champagne.

It was several months after this that he made the acquaintance of General Whiffletree, whom he had often seen in the different saloons and cafés which he frequented, and whose sayings and doings were chronicled with much frequency in the journals of the day, coupled with complimentary remarks about "that prince of good fellows," or "that well-known wit and *raconteur*," or "that genial veteran and peerless after-dinner talker." Dolly had noticed—for his brain did work in a way—that while the leading newspapers of the town differed with one another in regard to the faults and virtues of the dominant men of the day, they were unanimous in their praise of General Whiffletree, a fact which he deemed convincing proof that the General was the wittiest and cleverest, as well as the most distinguished and in every respect admirable man, in New York.

It was therefore with feelings of intense gratification that Dolly found himself seated across the table from the renowned warrior in the hotel café one cheerless winter afternoon, in company with a gentleman named Judge Doonothing, whose acquaintance he had made since his arrival in the city, and who enjoyed in the contemporary press a reputation only second to that of the General for cleverness and *bonhomie.*

Now General Whiffletree had had his eye on Dillenbeck for some weeks, and the acquaintance promised a great deal more for him than for the younger man; so he greeted him with an air of pompous, ceremonious politeness of the kind usually attributed by reporters to "gentlemen of the old school," in acknowledgment of which Dolly bowed profoundly, and then with some nervousness invited both gentlemen to sit down and join him.

Judge Doonothing, who was also a gentleman of the old school, because he had an enormous paunch and a ponderous manner, and wore a pair of gold-rimmed eye-glasses astride a red and bulbous nose, had no objection to sitting down with his young friend for a moment or two; and by a fortunate chance the General found himself at liberty for a short period also.

Dolly proudly tapped the bell and bade the waiter bring a bottle of Extra Dry, "and see that it's cold."

"I could have told you as much, General," remarked the Judge, with an air of resignation. "This young man will always insist upon buying wine, no matter what happens."

"Ah!" said the General, approvingly, "it is gratifying indeed to meet young men of the present generation who have the tastes of gentlemen. In our salad days, Judge, no gentleman ever thought of offering such a vulgar drink as beer to his friends about the festal board. If I were to offer a word of advice to Mr. Dillenbeck—and it seems to me that he hardly needs it—it would be to stick to champagne, the drink for gentlemen, sir."

Little did General Whiffletree think of the effect that his words had on the young man for whom they were intended. Dolly had come over to upper Broadway with no purpose save that of enjoyment; but during the weeks which had elapsed since his arrival he had learned from his intercourse with the class that fills the cafés and patrols the sidewalks of that part of the town that there was one career open to him in which he might reasonably hope to win distinction; and the remark of General Whiffletree—peerless wit, genial *raconteur*, popular veteran, etc.—settled at once a half-formed resolution that had been gathering strength in his mind ever since he first entered upon his inheritance.

In the brief period of time which elapsed between the ordering of the champagne and its appearance on the table, Dolly Dillenbeck determined that he would become a "wine-opener."

It may be that some of my readers do not know what a wine-opener is. For their benefit I would explain that it is one of the peculiar products of American civilization—a biped whose sole aim in life is to be known as a "perfect gentleman," and who sees but one path leading to the goal of his ambition. That path is strewn with empty bottles, headaches, heel-taps, scraps of tin-foil, and wire and corkscrews. The corks which he leaves behind him in his mad course are gathered up by the waiters and redeemed at twenty-five cents apiece by the wine-agents who are enriched by his matchless folly. The wine-opener's only duty in life is to purchase bottles of champagne on every possible occasion, and serve them to the thirsty genials who will swarm about him so long as his money lasts, sounding his praises as they prey upon him, and calling upon Allah to witness that he is the "prince of good fellows," the "perfect gentleman," the one citizen with "sporting blood to his fingers' ends," who will buy wine at all hours of the day and night.

Dolly had not failed to remark the high esteem in which men of the wine-opening class were held by those who drank at their expense. Their jokes, he had noticed, were always received with uproarious laughter and loud slapping of knees; while their stories, no matter how long or tedious they might be, commanded an almost reverent attention. Even such a famous wit as Judge Doonothing, who was usually so engrossed in his own conversation that he could pay scant heed to that of other people, never failed to catch the point of a wine-opener's story or joke and reward it with the tribute of hearty laughter.

And he had observed, too, that men whose mental and moral endowments were of the most commonplace description could always invest themselves with the finest and noblest qualities vouchsafed to erring humanity by the simple though rather costly process of gathering a half dozen of the *habitués* of the café about them and treating them to champagne. On such festive occasions he had not been blind to the fact that the rare personal charms of the host, his graceful bearing, his ready wit, his generosity, and his sensitive, noble nature were frequently made the subject of the most fulsome panegyrics, in which every one present heartily joined; and that in order to divert the conversation into this agreeable channel it was only necessary for the wine-opener to say, "Gentlemen, you can't spend a cent in this house to-night; everything is with me."

Having been an eye-witness of these strange phenomena, it is not to be wondered at that Dolly Dillenbeck should have debated within himself the propriety of becoming a wine-opener on a scale of such magnitude as had never before been attempted by any gudgeon on upper Broadway, or that the chance remark of such a distinguished man of the world as General Whiffletree should have crystallized his inchoate ideas into a fixed resolution. He determined to lose no time in embarking on his career, and by the time he had reached his fourth bottle he felt sure, from the complimentary remarks of his guests, and the deep respect with which they listened to his own stories and feeble attempts at repartee, that he was already rising rapidly in their estimation.

General Whiffletree seemed to take a great fancy to him, for the very next day he learned from no less than three disinterested acquaintances that that war-scarred veteran had declared in the presence of a large assemblage of genials that that young Mr. Dillenbeck was a "thoroughbred from the ground up," and that so long as his (the General's) "wad" held out, he (Dolly) should never want for a friend.

But what happened several months ago is ancient history in a gay, theatric career such as our hero entered upon under the competent guidance of General Whiffletree. Let us take up the thread of our story again, and see what has become of the young girl with the wide-open blue eyes, who disappeared into a Fourth Avenue horse-car, pausing on the platform to cast one look at the giddy, dashing youth who stood gazing hopelessly after her.

That single glance, aimed from the rear platform of a prosaic, every-day horse-car, hit the grinning, complacent, overdressed gudgeon on the sidewalk on his most vulnerable spot,—his vanity,—and made this story possible. If it had not been for that backward look. But this is no place for idle speculation. Let us go on with our romance.

## CHAPTER IV

At a corner table in the café of the St. Anthony House sat General Whiffletree, with a half-finished cocktail before him, an open letter in his hand, and on his face an expression in which rage, mortification, and an awful terror were comically blended. For nearly two hours he had been waiting for Dolly Dillenbeck, with whom he had an engagement for dinner and the theater, and the half-finished cocktail in front of him was the fourth he had ordered during that time. His change of countenance as he read the note brought him by a district messenger was so noticeable that the waiter, whom he had been bullying for an hour and a quarter, promptly placed a check for eighty cents on the table and stationed himself just within his range of vision. The letter which had stirred the old warrior's soul to its muddy depths was as follows:

"Sorry to disappoint you; but I have something on hand to-night which I really can't let slip, so I must ask you to put off our dinner till to-morrow,—same time and place,—when I will explain everything. *The girl we saw at Forty-second Street the other day is with me at this very minute.* How is that for quick work?

"In haste,

"DOLLY."

General Whiffletree laid the note on the table, and just then his eye fell on the check for the four cocktails.

"Who told you to bring that document to me?" he demanded, scowling ferociously at the waiter.

"The cashier, sir," responded the servitor, in a tone that was at once respectful and significant.

Now the General belonged to that large class of people who can look on without turning a hair while their friends settle bills of any amount, but are always thrown into paroxysms of fury when even the smallest bar check is brought to them for payment. For a moment he glared fiercely at the waiter, then pompously extracted the required amount from his vest-pocket, put on his hat and semi-military coat, and stalked indignantly out of the room. A quarter of an hour later he might have been seen entering a place of refreshment of a much humbler sort than the one he had just quitted. This one displayed in its front windows an appetizing array of yellow pumpkins, canned vegetables, and other indices of the fare provided within. From time to time the cheerful cries of the colored waiters echoed through the large, well-lighted dining-room. As the General seated himself at one of the small tables and carefully scrutinized the greasy bill of fare, he cursed himself for an infernal fool.

"What did I let that boy out of my sight for?" he demanded of his conscience. "If he falls into the clutches of that girl he'll be lost forever."

From which it may be inferred that the veteran had a keen sense of his duties as mentor, guide, and friend.

If the General could have seen the "boy" at that moment his disinterested anxiety for his welfare would not have perceptibly diminished; for Dolly was looking across a small dining-table directly into those dangerous blue depths, his face fairly beaming with triumph and delight at the thought that it was his irresistible powers of attraction, coupled with his tact as a man of the world, which had made her presence there with him possible.

He had met her quite accidentally that afternoon as he was taking his usual stroll up Broadway, and of course he had turned around and followed her; and she, not seeming to notice him, had turned into a side street and walked briskly toward the east, with her eager admirer clattering along about fifty paces behind her. Close to Lexington Avenue she had paused and looked up at the number on one of the houses, and then consulted a bit of paper in her hand with the air of one who had gone completely astray.

It was at this opportune moment that Dolly had borne down upon her, and, trembling at his own audacity, had stopped and asked if he could be of any service to her.

Indeed he could, for she was a stranger in the city, and was trying to find the house in which she had taken a room but two days before. Perhaps he would be good enough to direct her to the place,—she had it carefully written out on a little piece of paper,—and indeed it was very kind of him to take so much trouble for a perfect stranger. Was she really five blocks out of the way? And would she allow him to walk with her to the street in which she lived? She would be very grateful to him for the kindness. And so skilfully did our hero play his cards during that brief walk that at seven o'clock he found himself seated opposite to her in the way I have already described.

And he had learned from her own lips that she was a simple country maiden who had just come to New York, and that her name was Maude Wheatleigh.

He had "arrived" at last. His dream of years was realized. There was no ostrich plume waving above the sweet young face that looked up into his, but the smile was there, and the blue eyes were brighter and deeper than any that he had ever looked into before.

"Do you know," said the blue-eyed one, glancing about her with a look of trusting timidity, "that I am frightened almost to death when I think of being here all alone with a man I've known such a very short while! If I wasn't sure from your looks that you were a perfect gentleman I'd never dare do what I'm doing now; but somehow every few minutes I make up my mind I'll get up from the table and run right back home, I'm so afraid something awful will happen."

"Don't talk so, I beg of you," cried Dolly, placing a detaining hand on her wrist, and experiencing a distinct thrill of rapture when he found that she allowed it to remain there. "I assure you on my honor as a gentleman, Miss Wheatleigh, that if you will only put trust in me no harm shall befall you. We'll go to the theater to-night, and then I'll take you home and leave you there."

"How good you are!" she exclaimed impetuously, throwing a soulful look across the table at him. And then she fell to toying with her empty glass,—using her free hand, not the one which Dolly was now rapturously pressing,—and presently she said, "How do you call this sweet drink that foams? I think it's real nice."

"That," replied Dillenbeck, grandly, "is champagne, and we'll have another bottle." With which he touched the bell in a lordly fashion, while a very slight smile played across Miss Wheatleigh's lips.

They went to the theater that night—not to one of the fashionable playhouses, but to see a melodrama, which was drawing immense audiences at one of the big "combination houses," where it was billed for a week. It was an Irish melodrama of the good old sort, in which the villain reveals his sinister proclivities in the first act by attempting to collect the rents which are his lawful due—the worst form of infamy known to the Irish stage. There was also a scene in which the heroine met the villain by appointment at midnight in front of the old ruined mill, and, having indignantly refused to marry him, was promptly seized and incarcerated in an old stone tower by the lake-side. This tower was constructed after the old Celtic fashion, with walls of wire gauze, which afforded a view of the unfortunate maiden during the period of her captivity.

Maude Wheatleigh paid deep attention to the drama, and even her companion, who had at first assumed the *blasé* air of a man of the world, joined in the wild applause when the funny man, who had been an unobserved witness of the seizure of the heroine, rowed in a boat to the foot of the gauze tower and rescued her with the aid of a convenient rope-ladder, making his escape just in time to elude the villain, who stood on the shore shaking his riding-crop at the fugitives in impotent rage till the curtain hid him from view. They both rejoiced when the true will was found and the vast Fitzgerald-Fogarty estates were restored to their rightful owner, the heroine, to the unbounded delight of the peasantry, who knew that she was opposed on principle to the iniquitous practice of rent-collecting.

As they were slowly walking away after the final fall of the curtain Maude said, with a repetition of the timorous, trustful manner which she had already found so effective, "Mr. Dillenbeck, there's one thing I've been thinking about for a long time, and I'd like to ask your advice about it, if you don't mind, for somehow I feel that I have found in you a friend I can trust."

"Indeed you have; go right on and tell me what you want," exclaimed Dolly, impetuously.

"Well," continued the young girl, in hesitating tones, "I think I would like to be an actress; for I'm sure I would succeed if I only had a chance. Now don't you think you could help me? You know so many managers and people like that, while I know no one. And besides, you must have a great deal of influence, too; I'm sure you could do anything you wished with your persuasive, nice ways."

"My dear girl," he cried, completely won by her subtle flattery, "I'll be only too happy to do anything I can for you. I know several managers, and I'll see one of them the first thing to-morrow and try and get an opening for you. I've no doubt you'd be a big success; anyway, I'm sure you're a great deal better looking than any of those girls we saw to-night, and that ought to count for something."

"No flattery, now; that's against the rules," she retorted, tapping him playfully on the arm. And just then they reached her house, and she hastily bade him good-night and went in, leaving him to walk home in a state of exaltation which far exceeded anything that his favorite tipple could induce.

## CHAPTER V

BRIGHT and early the next morning, or rather at a few minutes before twelve, which is bright and early for a young *viveur* like Dolly, our hero entered the office of the famous theatrical firm of Hustle & Hardup, and inquired for the senior partner, whom he had frequently met in the St. Anthony café. Mr. Hustle, who was at that moment gloomily wondering where the money was to come from to tide him over the next salary day, took him at once into his private office and offered him a cigar. His face brightened perceptibly, and his thoughts took a more sanguine turn as the simple-minded youth unfolded to him his scheme for securing a position in some first-rate theatrical company for a young lady whom he knew slightly,—"simply as a friend, you understand,"—and who, in his judgment, possessed talents which were sure to make her a success.

Mr. Hustle listened with deep attention to all that Dolly had to say, and then asked for a few moments' time for reflection. In exactly two minutes—during which time he had calculated that five hundred dollars was about the proper sum to ask for—he informed his visitor that he happened to know of an exceptional opportunity for a young lady, provided she was pretty and clever. Of course if she was a novice it would be necessary for her to take some special lessons in dramatic art, but it was absolutely essential that she should possess beauty and cleverness.

Now Mr. Hustle's reasoning powers had been developed, by long friction with some of the craftiest scoundrels on Broadway, to a degree that would have excited the envy of a professor of logic in a German university; and he argued that if the girl were not pretty, Dolly would not take any interest in her; if not clever, then she would not know enough to enlist his services; and that if, possessing either or both of these qualities, she had had any experience on the stage, she would get an engagement herself, and in some company *not* under the management of Messrs. Hustle & Hardup, who were not famous for promptness or liberality in the payment of salaries.

"Could you bring her here this afternoon?" inquired Mr. Hustle when he had learned from the lips of his caller that the young lady was not only pretty, but "bright as a new dollar."

He could; and so it was arranged that Maude should call at two o'clock and her sponsor at five, which would give Mr.

Hustle time for consultation with his partner.

The senior member of the firm was alone in his private office when Dolly presented himself at the hour agreed upon and demanded in a tone of feverish eagerness which lifted Mr. Hustle's estimate from five hundred to eight hundred dollars, what he thought of Miss Wheatleigh.

"Oh, *she's* all right, my boy," said the manager, confidently. "She's not only pretty, but she's chock-full of talent. I only wish I'd got hold of her two weeks ago. We might have done something for her then, but now—"

"Why, I thought you told me this morning that you had an opening for a pretty and talented young girl!"

"That's just what I thought myself, my boy; but when I came to talk about it to Hardup he would n't listen to it for a minute, on account of the expense. It's like pulling teeth to get a cent out of him, no matter how promising the venture may be. Now I'm just the other way—always willing to take chances when I see a good thing; and I've been long enough in the business to know a good thing when I see it. The very minute I set eyes on Miss Wheatleigh I see she was a winner; and so far as I'm concerned I'd take the risk in a minute, and put her in a part where she'd stand some chance of making a hit. Even now I've got just enough confidence in that lady's talent to make her an offer—not the one I hoped to make her when I saw you this morning, but a good offer for a beginner. We're sending out a company in a week or two to play the Pacific coast, and I'm willing—"

"The Pacific coast! Why, she'd be away for six months at the very least!" cried Dolly, with a look of despair that made the manager bite his lips hard to keep from laughing outright.

"Six months!" he continued. "Why, if the company catches on we're thinking of sending them to Honolulu and over the Australian circuit."

The young man's face fell, and he shook his head so lugubriously that Mr. Hustle was obliged to step to the door and make a pretense of speaking to one of the clerks in order to hide his mirth.

"Well, I'm afraid that's the best I can do," he remarked as he returned to his seat. "You see, Hardup is always kicking about expense, and trying to cut everything down to hard-pan. My idea was to put this little lady into a very nice speaking part in the piece we're going to bring out next month; have her coached for it by some first-class instructor, get her some fine dresses, and spend a little money with the newspaper boys, you know, just to make sure that she got a fair show before the public. Let's see; we open in Paterson about five weeks from to-day, and about a month or two after that we're due at the Jollity Theater here in New York. It's my opinion that by that time she'll have made such progress that she'll take the town by storm—yes, sir, by storm. But the expense, my boy, is something awful, and my partner won't hear of it."

"How much would it cost?" demanded Dolly.

"It would cost," continued the manager, thoughtfully rubbing his chin, "at least a thousand dollars, and it might—"

"Very well," said the victim, "I'll foot the bill myself; but it's on condition that nothing shall be known about my connection with the enterprise."

"My dear boy," said Mr. Hustle, suavely, but in a tone of reproach, "do you think that anything that happens in this office is ever known outside? I only hope that you will be as careful not to mention the transaction as I shall be; for if it ever became known on Broadway that we were taking money from outside parties, our credit would be seriously damaged."

So it was settled that Miss Wheatleigh should begin her studies the next day under the direction of Mr. Horatio Rungdown, the celebrated Shakespearian actor, whom Mr. Dillenbeck had frequently entertained in the St. Anthony café, and for whose talents he entertained a profound respect. It was also arranged that the check for one thousand dollars, drawn to the order of Messrs. Hustle & Hardup, should be delivered up at the same time; and with this understanding Dolly departed to keep his engagement with General Whiffletree.

He had barely reached the staircase when he found that he had forgotten his umbrella; and on going back for it he was amazed to find Messrs. Hustle & Hardup waltzing madly around the little private office, overthrowing chairs, bumping into desks, and threatening at each turn to demolish the glass partitions. They stopped abruptly when they saw him standing in the doorway, and Mr. Hustle advanced with perfect *sang-froid* and said, "That's the dance for the second act of the new piece your lady friend is going to make her début in. Hardup invented it, and when we've practised it a bit together we'll teach it to the people. What do you think of it?"

Dolly found his military friend in rather bad humor and very much on his dignity. "If I had known earlier in the day that you were not coming," he remarked pompously, "I would have accepted the invitation of my old friend Senator Hardscrabble to dine and pass the evening at his hotel; but not hearing from you, I waited here till long after seven o'clock, and nearly caught my death in a confounded draft." The only draft there was the one on his vest-pocket, which had cost him precisely eighty cents.

The news of Dolly's meeting with Maude Wheatleigh, and of his efforts to put her on the stage (nothing was said of the check to Hustle & Hardup), did not tend to restore the General's good-humor; for he saw in the young woman only a possible rival, and he wished, for purely personal reasons, to retain his place as chief friend and adviser to the fortunate youth who had half a million in his pockets and no ambition except to become a celebrated wine-opener.

"You'd better be careful," he said ominously, as Dolly finished his recital. "These actresses get a man into a heap of trouble sometimes, and there's precious little good comes from knowing them. Once you begin putting up for them there's no end to their demands. They'd wear sealskin sacques in August for the sake of having you pay for them."

"Oh, I can take care of myself; they've got to get up pretty early in the morning to get the best of me," was the gilded youth's jaunty reply to the very first bit of good counsel the General had ever given him.

# CHAPTER VI

As I read over what I have written it seems to me that I should pause at this point in my story—perhaps I should have done so before—and tell my readers something about my pretty blue-eyed heroine, whom I fear I have injured in the estimation of those excellent people of conventional and sober modes of life and thought who would see in what I have told of her conduct with my young hero nothing but a gross and inexcusable violation of the proprieties.

That Miss Wheatleigh made the acquaintance of Mr. Dillenbeck on a public street and accompanied him to the theater on the same evening is undeniably true, because I, who alone know all the important episodes of her career, have written it; but that I did her an unintentional wrong in describing that circumstance without first telling my readers something about her antecedents is also true, and I feel that I must hasten to repair the error, and, if possible, rehabilitate her in the estimation of those who have done me the honor of reading my narrative.

Among the many parcels of real estate described in the schedule of the possessions of Jacob Dillenbeck, deceased, is the property known as Cold Brook Farm, situated on the old turnpike about midway between the towns of Maplefield and Millbridge, in a beautiful, hilly, well-wooded part of Massachusetts. To this farm the Dillenbecks were wont to come for the summer months; and as they were among the very few New-Yorkers of any wealth who possessed homes in that region, they were known by sight to every one who dwelt within a dozen miles of them. A few, indeed, knew them personally, and used to exchange greetings with them on Sundays at the Congregational church in Maplefield, or on week-days if they chanced to meet them driving along the country roads or shopping in the village stores.

They were not fond of society, however; and although it was agreed on all sides that they were homely and unpretentious folk, and not at all " stuck up," it was also generally known that they were people who liked to keep to themselves, and were particularly solicitous of their only son, whose only playmate was young Joe Whitcomb, the son of the pastor of the church which they attended.

Now in the little town of Millbridge, distant about five miles from the Cold Brook Farm, there lived a widow named Hunt and her daughter Polly. Mrs. Hunt owned the little old gray house in which she lived, and, with the help of a sister who was in fairly good circumstances, had contrived to feed and clothe herself and her daughter until the latter was old enough to add by her labor to the family income. At eighteen Polly went to Maplefield to learn the trade of dressmaking; and as she was a girl of much cleverness and beauty, it was not long before she attracted the favorable notice of a score or more of the young men who were looked upon by the other girls in the shop as the most desirable sweethearts within their reach.

Now Maplefield had a population of nearly ten thousand souls; and Polly soon found, to her intense mortification, that in the social strata into which its inhabitants were divided, the layer to which she and her fellow-workers of the dressmaker's shop and the young clerks who admired them belonged was one that did not enjoy a very high rank in the community. In Millbridge, a mere scattered hamlet of not more than two hundred houses, among which her mother's modest and time stained home was not below the average in point of cost and comfort, she had always felt herself to be as good as any of her neighbors, and decidedly better than most of them. She had taken the place in the Maplefield dressmaker's shop principally because of the social advantages which she believed she would enjoy there. She had exhausted her native village, and she expected that Maplefield would enlarge her knowledge of the world and prepare her in a way for some career—she did not know precisely what—that would enable her to become some one of importance in some great city like Boston or New York.

Her father, whom she scarcely remembered, had been a house- and sign-painter, and from him Polly had inherited a distinctly artistic temperament.

I must either explain my last sentence or else try to put my meaning in some other form. It bears a very close resemblance to the sort of sentence that occurs frequently in professedly humorous stories, and is introduced as a sort of hallmark to guarantee the fact that the manuscript in which it is embedded is really humorous in purpose and achievement. The dullest bumpkin that ever edited the humorous page of a Sunday newspaper knows that it is funny to say that an artistic temperament has been inherited from a house- and sign-painter; and although he may not have the remotest idea as to what an artistic temperament is, confidence in the comical nature of the story is greatly enhanced, and he is liable to publish and pay for it.

Therefore it behooves me to explain that when I mentioned the source of Polly Hunt's artistic inheritance I merely stated a simple truth and had no intention of being funny. Joe Hunt had possessed an artistic nature, which had found rude ex-

"TO THE SUCCESS OF A CERTAIN YOUNG LADY—"

pression in many quaintly lettered signs that may still be seen in front of the shops in Maplefield and Millbridge. He had possessed, also, in a still more marked degree, a deep love of nature, a passion for watching the flights of birds and studying the habits of the rabbit and the fox. He would follow the course of a trout-stream from dawn to dusk, and lie for hours at a time on his back beneath the forest-trees looking up at the floating clouds and the patches of blue sky, and vaguely regretting that he was what he was.

Now, as every one knows, nothing is more thoroughly incompatible with the art or trade of money-getting than a deep love of nature. I doubt if I have ever known a man who had amassed a fortune and who really enjoyed the woods and the fields. A rich man, it is true, usually contrives to purchase, at some prosperous moment, a more or less pretentious country-seat; and I have noticed that in nine cases out of ten he devotes a great deal of money and the entire energy of his declining years to the task of disfiguring his domain and rendering it, if possible, more hideous and vulgar than the neighboring properties on which his fellow-plutocrats are doing their worst.

His artistic sense first finds adequate expression in stone walls which are built to mark the confines of his estate.

There are plenty of stone walls on the farms about him, made of rough boulders piled one on top of another, and rendered beautiful by rank growths of trailing vines and moss; but his stone walls are of hewn stone and cement, with no green growing thing to soften their hard outlines, and suggestive of a prison rather than of lawn and garden. Hideous tinned or whitened statues of naked heathen deities spring up about his mansion. An artificial grotto with a cascade of real water—which issues from a real leaden pipe, and may be turned on or off by means of a stop-cock — rears itself at some point where it would be impossible for a grotto or a living spring to exist; and then a German horticulturist adds his conception of what is ornamental in landscape-gardening to the work of desecrating the fair earth.

Outraged nature finds her only solace in the knowledge that the artificial cave and cascade — a decorative impertinence which no word in the English tongue can fittingly describe — are known as a "rockery."

The grassy door-yard of the old gray farm-house that sheltered Joe Hunt's family was cool and inviting with its shade of maple and scent of lilac-blossoms. The lawn in front of the house in which Jacob Dillenbeck "resided" — the Hunts were poor and merely "lived" in theirs — was kept trimmed down to the quick by the sharp teeth of the mower, while the narrow strip along the roadway and outside the stone wall looked like an Irish laborer's upper lip after the Sunday-morning shave.

A famous artist once stopped at Mrs. Hunt's door to ask for a drink of water, and remained to sketch the old well-curb, from which a brown path led through deep green grass to the kitchen door where Polly stood watching the painter and knowing the while that he was drawing her as well as the rest.

The same artist passed the Dillenbeck estate later in the day with averted face and a groan of disgust on his lips.

It was from this house- and sign-painter, who loved the woods and streams, and was not unconscious of the restful beauty of his own modest home, that Polly inherited her artistic nature. To her practical, sharp New England mother she owed the self-reliance, ambition, and determination to conquer which served to render her impatient of her commonplace surroundings in Maplefield, and later exerted a marked influence on her career.

She soon wearied of the silly chatter of the other young women who worked beside her in the dressmaker's shop, and, greatly to their relief, declined to receive the attentions of the young men with whom they consorted. It was considered an evidence of very poor taste on her part that she should prefer to spend an evening poring over some novel taken from the circulating library rather than take part in a "straw-ride," or attend the monthly meeting of the Mineola Social Club; but it was in these books that she found her only real enjoyment. They were for the most part novels and story-books of the kind that are usually sneered at as "trashy" or "sensational," but which are in reality blessed above all other writings, inasmuch as they have lifted up so many worn and weary souls from the dull round of this work-a-day life to the realms that are peopled by the children of romance.

It was during this novel-reading period of her life that Polly Hunt happened to see the handsome and well-dressed youth who was wont to spend his summers at the Cold Brook Farm. He came into the dressmaking shop one morning in company with his mother, and seemed ill enough at ease under the keen glances that were turned toward him from every part of the room. Polly stared at him along with the rest, and at the first glance her work fell from her hands and a bright-red spot burned on each of her cheeks, while her breath came in quick, short gasps. It seemed to her that she saw before her in the flesh the young Earl of Redfernne, from whom she had parted that very morning before breakfast just as his father's younger brother was about to imprison him in a damp dungeon beneath Audrey Towers.

Dolly Dillenbeck was an exceedingly good-looking young chap at that time, and it was not at all strange that he should precisely fill out the ideal already formed in the brain of the romantic young shop-girl of the aristocratic heir to Audrey Towers and the Redfernne earldom.

"My, just look at Polly! She looks as if something had struck her all of a sudden," snickered one of the girls as Mrs. Dillenbeck and her son left the shop. The color on Miss Hunt's cheeks became an angry scarlet as she picked up her work from the floor and resumed her sewing amid a chorus of suppressed giggling; for her companions were all glad enough of a chance to ridicule the "stuck-up thing" who thought herself too good to associate with them.

Polly bore their teasings for a time, and then blurted out, "Well, when I have a beau it will be Mr. Dillenbeck, or some one that's just as stylish as him; and I could have him, too, if I chose to set my cap for him, you 'd better believe."

"My, what a big tail our cat 's got!" chirruped the girl who had started the subject, and who was the wit of the shop.

"I suppose you 're content with a chalk-faced, knock-kneed counter-jumper who has to hop every time he hears any one holler 'Ca-a-a-a-sh,'" retorted Polly. And the other said no more, for her particular "feller" was a pallid youth who found employment in the One Price Dry-goods Emporium, and took his walks abroad with a springy wabble in his gait.

The next day it was reported on Main Street that that pretty Hunt girl who worked at Miss Thimbleton's had declared her intention to "make up" to the heir of Cold Brook Farm and heaven alone knew how many millions of dollars besides; and the rumor flew until it reached the ears of Mrs. Dillenbeck's maid, who promptly repeated it to her mistress, thereby filling her soul with an awful dread.

She instantly made up her mind that something must be done to prevent the young "hussy" from carrying out her designs on Dolly, who was one of the few persons in the neighborhood who was still unaware of them; for the news had spread with the rapidity characteristic of a leisurely, quick-witted, gossip-loving community.

Mrs. Dillenbeck found it convenient to call at the dressmaker's a day or two later, and it was an easy matter for her to identify Polly, who was hard at work with her needle, and apparently oblivious of the presence of the visitor and the significant smiles and glances of her associates.

Mrs. Dillenbeck went home feeling that her fears had been only too well founded, and that either her son or the designing young shop-girl must be removed to a safe distance. Polly was a "hussy"—there could be no doubt of that. She had suspected it as soon as she heard of her, and a single look had sufficed to convince her that her surmise had been correct.

In the vocabulary of women of the Mrs. Dillenbeck type a "hussy" merely signifies a woman who is pretty or interesting enough to attract the attention of some man who ought to be occupied in some other way. It was late in September, and she thought that a six weeks' stay at the seashore would be an excellent thing for both Dolly and herself. That would dispose of the vexing question until the next summer at least.

The same busybody who had told Mrs. Dillenbeck's maid about the Hunt girl's threat now learned from that domestic the true reason for the sudden departure of the family nearly two months before their usual time, and made haste to impart the information to the innocent cause of all the trouble.

Polly's eyes glistened with delight—what girl's would not?—when she learned that she, who had been utterly ignored by Maplefield society, was considered by the wealthy and reserved Mrs. Dillenbeck to possess beauty and other attractive personal qualities in a degree that rendered her dangerous to the safety and well-being of the best-looking and most eligible young man in the county. It was the first great triumph of her life, and one that she enjoyed far more keenly than any that came to her in the eventful years that were so soon to follow.

Through the autumn and well into the winter Polly toiled industriously with her needle. Then her mother sickened and died, and, as soon as the affairs of the widow's little estate had been settled, the daughter accepted a position in one of the largest of the New England cities; for

Maplefield had grown more and more intolerable to her with every succeeding month. She remained nearly a year in her new home, living prudently and discreetly, and yet finding time to make a few acquaintances and enlarge her sphere of observation. She made one or two trips to New York during this period, acting as a buyer for her employer, and enjoying with splendid zest the great panorama of metropolitan life that revealed itself to her in the streets and in the theater, to which she went under the escort of the drummer from whom she bought dry-goods with a shrewdness and caution that commanded his immediate respect even while it reduced his profit on the transaction.

Her first day in New York convinced her that she had not been intended for life in a small town or provincial city, where the fact that she had begun life as a sewing-girl would always stand in the way of her success. Her friend the drummer pointed out to her the houses of some of the richest and most famous men in the town, and told her how much money it had cost to build them, and how many millions of dollars had been accumulated by their owners. She learned from him, also, that in nearly every case the fortune whose outward and visible sign was a stately monument in brick or stone standing on some broad avenue or quiet and aristocratic side-street had come from the very smallest beginnings. This man had begun life as an errand-boy in a big warehouse; his neighbor had been a driver of mules on the tow-path of the Erie Canal; while a third had actually sold dry-goods at retail, had been a mere "counter-jumper"—in fact, one of the same class from which the Maplefield shop-girls took their beaus.

It must be a wonderful city, she thought, in which the poor and the lowly can not only achieve such splendid success, but afterward be allowed to enjoy the result of their labors. In smaller communities the tow-path and the ribbon-counter would never be either forgiven or forgotten, while in New York they were regarded as a matter of course. "One of these days," she said to herself, "I will live in one of these beautiful houses, and then the fact that I was once a sewing-girl in a dressmaker's shop will never be thrown in my face."

One day, Polly Hunt, acting on a sudden and irresistible impulse, threw up her position, packed up her belongings, and started for New York. As she emerged from the Grand Central Depot she saw and recognized Dolly Dillenbeck; and the glance which she threw at him from the platform of the Fourth Avenue horse-car was a distinct bid on her part for his acquaintance.

She changed her name on arriving in

the city, in pursuance of a determination already formed to put the old life completely behind her and embark on some career—the stage seemed to her the most feasible—which would give scope to whatever artistic talents she might possess.

It was by accident that she met Dolly on Broadway, and, knowing perfectly well who he was, she felt that it was right and proper for her to accept his invitation to dinner. After all, she was alone and friendless, and must avail herself of every advantage that came her way.

# CHAPTER VII

When Polly Hunt—who will be known in the pages to follow as Maude Wheatleigh—after a short period of instruction under that eminent Shakespearian scholar and actor, Mr. Horatio Rungdown, joined the Hustle & Hardup combination she fully realized that one of the great opportunities of her life lay before her, and she resolved to improve it to the very best of her ability. Her début was made in a small town where the company appeared but one night, and she filled a very small rôle. The event attracted about as much attention in the artistic world as the advent of another fly in a slaughter-house, but she was not disappointed. She did not wish to become known as the exponent of insignificant parts, and she had sense enough to regard this period of her career as one of valuable schooling. Besides, Mr. Hustle had promised her that Mr. Freelance, who was to join the company shortly and travel with it for a time as a sort of general factotum, would strengthen her part and write some lines especially for her.

Of course Dolly was present on the occasion of her début, and he wondered, as he glanced around the house, if she seemed to the audience as pretty and fascinating as she did to him. For Maude was pretty and fascinating, and clever into the bargain—so much so, in fact, that the leading juvenile lady wanted to know, on more than one occasion, why Mr. Hustle would persist in filling up the company with clumsy amateurs.

Her talent and good looks made an instant impression on Mr. Freelance the first time he saw the play, and in his letter to the managers the next day he expressed his belief that in engaging her they had builded better than they knew. In the mean time, he said, he would develop her part, rehearse her in it, and give her a chance to show what she amounted to. All of which was an agreeable surprise to Messrs. Hustle & Hardup, who had engaged her simply and solely because of Dolly Dillenbeck and his thousand dollars.

Mr. Freelance was a young man of diversified talents and erratic tendencies. In a theater he was simply invaluable, because he could make himself useful in a hundred different ways. He could rewrite an act or strengthen a part; he could write topical verses at a moment's notice; and when it came to composing romances about the principal members of the company, to be used for advertising purposes, it was acknowledged on all sides that he was without a superior. A dozen times had he been in the employ of Hustle & Hardup, and a dozen times had they quarreled and separated, only to come together again a month or two later. Those eminent managers literally swore by him, because in addition to the traits I have already mentioned he was a passed master in both the theory and the practice of strategic finance.

There was general rejoicing on the night of Mr. Freelance's arrival from New York; and when, at the close of the second act, he made his way to the region behind the footlights, the members of the company crowded about him, each one eager for an opportunity to air some grievance or to get inside information about the financial condition of Hustle & Hardup, and the prospects of the ghost's walking regularly during the tour. To these inquiries Mr. Freelance responded in a jubilant, confident manner which served to prop up the spirits of the actors to a wonderful degree, which was precisely the effect that both he and his employers had calculated on.

He had a few words with our heroine, and told her that he intended to change her part and give her a little more to do — information which raised her to the seventh heaven of delight.

Mr. Freelance was as good as his word. He began work on the part of *Polly Lightfoot* the very next day, and by Sunday he had materially altered the dialogue of the second act in order to give it due prominence. The consequences of this act were described in a long letter to Mr. Hustle, in which he said:

"As I told you before, that girl has great natural talent and is making wonderful progress. Perhaps there was n't a row when I gave out the parts for the revised second act! I could hear the cries of the wounded a block off. We played the new version last night, and it was a great improvement, though none of the others think so, because it gives Wheatleigh a good deal of the fat. She got a curtain-call at the close of the act, and went out and took it as if she 'd been starring for twenty years instead of 'soubretting' for six weeks. You ought to have seen Pearl Livingstone's face when Wheatleigh took her call. Upon my soul, I believe we could get rid of that cat and put the other little girl in her part.

"How about that moon-faced dude who put up the thousand bones? Don't let him drop off the hook, for we may want to touch him again; and besides, if his protégée does as well as I think she will, he might be induced to back her for a starring tour, and I honestly believe there 's money in it. Sound him on the subject, and remember one thing: he 's just ripe now, and ready to fall off the limb; and if you don't pick him pretty soon somebody else will. I hear he 's making his ducats fly pretty fast as it is—I know he dropped four thousand of them in one night just because he got an anonymous letter saying that the double naught was going to turn up thirty-five times in two hours and a half. Will these suckers *ever* tumble to anything?

"But, whatever you do, don't let that old fraud, Rungdown, give her any more lessons in dramatic art. I've had to make her unlearn everything he taught her, and show her how to read her lines myself. I will write you again in a few days and send you papers from Cleveland and Pittsburg, provided we get any good notices."

One evening a few weeks after this letter was written, Dolly suddenly appeared in Troy, where the piece was billed for two nights; and accompanying him was General Whiffletree, who, having become very suspicious regarding his young friend's interest in the actress, had persuaded Dolly to bring him with him, in order, as he put it, that he might see for himself how much talent the young lady really possessed.

It was nearly eight o'clock when they

reached Troy. They drove at once to the theater, entering, as they thought, unobserved, and taking seats that were not conspicuous. But Mr. Freelance saw them, and a few minutes later the news spread through the dressing-rooms that Hustle's "angel" was in front, in company with a man who looked solid enough to back a grand opera company.

It may have been because of the presence of these distinguished visitors, possibly because of purely artistic fervor on the part of the actors; but at any rate the play was given that night with a degree of smoothness and vivacity that was simply unprecedented, and produced a favorable impression on the audience. As for Miss Wheatleigh, she fairly outdid herself; and when, at the close of the second act, she appeared timorously before the curtain, swept the house with a modest, smiling look, and then disappeared, Dolly was simply in ecstasy, and even the General admitted that she appeared to have some talent—"if it could only be properly cultivated."

A very proud man was our hero that night when he escorted the young actress into the hotel restaurant, where the General, with the dregs of his fourth cocktail before him, was awaiting them. And never, since the day of their first meeting, had Maude seemed as charming and agreeable as she was during the little supper that followed. She paid particular court to General Whiffletree, told him she was dying to hear some of his droll stories, and listened to everything he said with an expression of confiding, round-eyed reverence that not only made that battle-scarred veteran feel the fires of youth once more in his veins, but actually gave Dolly a twinge of jealousy.

"Well, what do you think of her?" inquired our hero as the two friends boarded the sleeping-car for New York.

The General was in that mellow and tender mood which can be best brought about by cocktails, champagne, and three or four ponies of brandy. "What do I think of her?" he repeated ponderously, as he deposited himself in one of the cushioned seats. "She's a winner, my boy; and if you were to put that woman on the road at the head of a company of her own she'd carry everything before her. And that, sir, is the opinion of a man who has been going to theaters for more years than you've been on earth, and has seen 'em all, from Rachel to Bernhardt. Is there a drop left in that flask of yours, Dolly? If there is, just hand it over here, will you?"

"You can keep it and give it to me when I see you in New York," cried Dolly, suddenly rising to his feet and buttoning his overcoat.

"What do you mean?" gasped the General.

"I mean that I'm going to stop here overnight. There's something I forgot to say to Freelance. Good-by."

"Hold on!" cried the fuddled warrior. "I'll get off and stay with you. I'll see you through, Dolly, if it costs a leg."

But Dolly had jumped from the already moving train before the old man could reach the car door, and as the cars rolled on toward the city they bore, among other live freight, the angry, suspicious, and surly General Whiffletree, who instantly vented his ill humor on the colored porter of the sleeping-car, thereby rendering it incompatible with his dignity to fee that respectful and diligent functionary the next morning.

Meantime Dolly was driving rapidly to the hotel in order to see Miss Wheatleigh before she went to bed. He found her in one of the reception-rooms talking with Mr. Freelance — she mentioned that he was merely instructing her in her rôle — and as soon as that invaluable factotum had departed she yawned and remarked that she was tired and sleepy.

"My dear," cried Dillenbeck, throwing his arm about her and boldly attempting to draw her toward him, "so am I tired and sleepy; but we 'll have just one bottle first, and then —"

In an instant the young girl was standing before him with flashing eyes and heaving breast.

"You dare to speak to me like that!" she exclaimed, looking down at him with an indignation which he literally did not dare to face. She stood for a single moment a picture of wounded virtue; then her lips quivered, she turned away, and, covering her face with both hands, burst into a flood of tears.

"My dear Miss Wheatleigh, I really assure you I had n't the least idea of saying anything that would offend you," cried our hero, in great alarm. "Now I beg of you—"

"Mr. Dillenbeck," exclaimed the young actress, in calm, measured tones, "leave me this instant!"

And poor Dolly took his hat and coat and slunk off, a picture of shame and dejection.

A few minutes later, as Miss Wheatleigh was unlocking the door of her room, Mr. Freelance emerged from the shadowy corridors and saluted her.

"That you, Billy?" she rejoined, in cheerful accents; for she had completely regained her equanimity by this time. "I'll tell you what I want you to do for me one of these days," she continued. "I want you to write a play with a star part of a girl who is called upon to rebuke the tempter, and who does it in great style, and at the same time does n't lose her grip on him. And I want to play that part."

"Been rehearsing it already, I suppose,"

remarked Mr. Freelance, with a faint show of interest.

"Good-night, Billy," was her only reply.

"Good-night, dear," said Mr. Freelance.

And then Maude went into her room and locked the door in a resolute, emphatic way that did not escape the notice of Mr. Hustle's accomplished business manager.

## CHAPTER VIII

ONE fine Saturday afternoon Dolly Dillenbeck stood at the corner of Broadway and Twenty-third Street talking to his old boyhood friend, Joe Whitcomb, now a sturdy, sensible, prosperous young man of business, who had just left his home in Maplefield for a short trip to New York. He had met and recognized his old playmate on Broadway, and the young metropolitan, whose heart had always been a healthier organ than his brain, was unfeignedly glad to see him, and to have an opportunity to show him round the city.

"What a lucky thing, old man, that I chanced to run across you!" he exclaimed as he took his old friend by the arm. "Now we'll just take a little walk up Broadway, and then we'll have dinner somewhere, and try to fill in the evening in one way or another. But remember, while you're traveling with me your money don't go. I've got a wad in my pocket you could n't make a dent in with a brick."

To do our hero justice, it must be said of him that he honestly rejoiced in the possession of wealth, and that his heart was filled with a generous desire to make all those with whom he came in contact sharers, to a certain extent, in his prosperity. But his vanity—which, after all, was of a simple, good-natured kind—was his ruling characteristic, and was the chief cause of the foolish excesses which had already made him a marked figure in those strata of society which crop out so abundantly along upper Broadway. He was sincere in his wish to entertain his old playmate to the very best of his ability, but at the same time he wished to impress upon him the fact that T. Adolphus Dillenbeck was a young man of some importance in the great metropolitan whirlpool. It would be something for him to have Joe Whitcomb go back to Maplefield and tell everybody about the easy and familiar way in which he (Dolly) took his afternoon stroll up Broadway, and how all the principal citizens whom he encountered recognized and saluted him.

As for Joe, he was only too glad to meet his old friend and see the town under his guidance; so he willingly turned his face to the north, and together they strolled up the famous thoroughfare. It was just three o'clock, and, as Dolly put it, the "mob was out in full force." Unknowingly he employed the very best word he could have found in the language to describe the crowd of people who pace or hurry or wander or walk up and down Broadway between Twenty-third and Thirty-third streets every fair afternoon. In no other place and at no other time does so much of the froth of the metropolis come to the surface.

The stranger who finds himself swept along in the current sees only well-groomed men and stylish and sometimes beautiful women, and from time to time catches a glimpse of a face that somehow seems familiar. If he be an observant man he will quickly notice a difference between this crowd and the one, for example, which patrols Fifth Avenue, just one block away. The crowd is much denser here; there are more men of spare build and keen, clear-cut profiles; and the women seem to him to be better dressed—though, as a matter of fact, they are not—than on Fifth Avenue.

There is another peculiarity about the current on Broadway, and he will become dimly conscious of it by the time he has mingled with it a week: and that is the quick, eager, searching glances which its component particles will flash into his face as he passes. On Fifth Avenue he will be noticed, if at all, either haughtily, smilingly, compassionately, or carelessly, according to his appearance; but all the looks directed toward him on Broadway will have the same significance—" Who is this new man? Is it worth our while to bother with him?"

Now, when the New-Yorker who knows and loves his Gotham with all her faults and all her beauties, as only a New-Yorker can, and as every New-Yorker should,— when such a one reaches upper Broadway on his afternoon walk he surveys the passing throng with a peculiar zest; and if he chance to have with him a stranger, he will point out to him the different men and women who have contrived to establish little separate eddies of their own in the frothy tide of city life. He will know the names of those whose faces have been in the public prints, and some who figure in the interesting photographic collection at Police Headquarters. The experienced

New-Yorker can tell at a glance the exact status of those striking-looking women who pass in and out of their carriages, or sit in the front windows of restaurants with overdressed men, looking out at the current of life and gossiping about the other men and women who pass by. He knows, too, the histories of a dozen or more of these people, and when he has told them to you over a cup of coffee and a cigar in a snug corner of some well-ordered restaurant you will wonder what force has served to bring them all together from so many distant corners of the earth to walk up and down that half-mile stretch on the same fine afternoon.

It was right into the midst of this froth that Dolly Dillenbeck plunged that bright afternoon, with Joe Whitcomb on his arm. Their first stop was at the St. Anthony Café, into which our hero sailed with an air of ownership which was not without its effect on his companion.

"Ah! how do, General!" he said, pleasantly, as he entered, and then added, in an undertone, "That's the celebrated General Whiffletree the newspapers make such a fuss about; you've heard about him, I'm sure."

"I don't quite recall him just now," replied Joe, dubiously. "What's he celebrated for?"

"Celebrated for!" retorted Dolly, annoyed that the mere mention of the veteran's name did not make a tremendous impression on his country friend. "Why, he's one of the best-known men in New York, a famous story-teller, knows everybody — regular man about town, in fact. You can't pick up a Sunday paper without seeing his picture in it, or else some story about him. Why, I thought everybody had heard of him."

"Oh!" remarked Joe, innocently or malevolently — Dolly did not know which; "I supposed from his title that he had made his reputation in the army. Yes, I'd like very much to meet him."

A moment later the three men were seated at a small round table, and Dolly was telling the waiter to bring a large bottle "and be quick about it."

"So you're up to your old tricks already, young man," said the General, shaking a jocose forefinger at his young host. "The best isn't too good for you, I see; nothing but wine will suit a high roller like you." Then, turning to Joe, he continued: "Your friend has been on the turf only a very short time, and yet there are very few of the old-timers who can hold a candle to him when it comes to setting up wine. I have seen that young man, sir," he went on, dropping his voice, but not too low for Dolly to hear—"I have seen him sit right here in this café and open twelve bottles one after another without turning a hair. He's got sporting blood in him all the way through."

The wine came, and close behind it lumbered Judge Doonothing. The pop of the cork awoke Mr. Rungdown, who was dozing peacefully in a warm corner. Both gentlemen seated themselves at Mr. Dillenbeck's invitation, and a moment later the company was augmented by Senator Hardscrabble and Dr. Puffe — both genials of the most pronounced type.

"You want to look out for this man Puffe, Mr. Whitcomb," said Judge Doonothing, waggishly. "He's one of these wicked newspaper fellers, and he's liable to write you up pretty near any time."

"He seems to have it in for me for some reason or 'nother," cried Dolly, merrily; "he gives me a shot in the paper about once a week. Say, Major, what have I ever done to you, anyway, that you should use me like that? Have n't I always used you right?"

"My dear boy," cried the scribe, stretching his long arm across the table and grasping and seizing his host's hand, "I have n't got a truer friend in this town than you. If I was to get into trouble to-day there 's nobody in New York I 'd go to for help quicker 'n I 'd go to you."

"And there 's nobody I know of who 'd go down deeper into his pocket to help a friend than the gentleman whose delightful hospitality we are enjoying just now, and I call upon you all to drink his health in brimming glasses; no heel-taps, remember." And amid a chorus of approval Mr. Rungdown replenished the glasses of the company, thus artfully paving the way for another bottle, which Dolly promptly ordered. They had already had three at his expense.

"See here, old man," cried Whitcomb, suddenly drawing a roll of bills from his vest pocket, "it 's somebody else's turn to buy a bottle now. Let me pay for this, and then if we have any more we 'll each put up in turn.—Don't you think that 's right?" he inquired, turning to Senator Hardscrabble, who sat at his left with his head bowed on his chest, dreaming the happy hours away in an imaginary game of draw.

"That's all right," said the statesman, cheerfully, "but it's my edge, remember that. I'm on the left of the dealer."

"That brings it on to you, General," continued Joe, taking up the Senator's idea; "raise the ante and the edge passes."

"I don't understand you, sir," replied the General, with much dignity. And then Dolly turned the conversation into other channels by saying positively, "Not a bit of it, Joe. I told you I had a wad, and while it holds out these gentlemen are my guests and I won't allow them to spend a cent."

But Joe's proposition to share the expense of the entertainment seemed to have cast a gloom over the company, and checked the tide of whole-souled geniality, bringing in its stead a feeling of unrest and apprehension similar to that which had prevailed on a certain memorable evening about three weeks before, when Judge Doonothing, while reaching across the table for a match, accidentally touched the bell and brought the waiter to the table on the dead run.

From the St. Anthony House the two friends strolled slowly uptown until they reached a small and handsomely furnished saloon much frequented by the hangers-on of the theatrical profession. A portly man, well advanced in years, who was seated at a table on which there was nothing but a match-box, saluted Dolly with eager cordiality as they entered.

"There's one of the best-known characters in New York," exclaimed Dolly, "and I think I'd better ask him over here to have a glass of wine with us."

"You seem to have a wide acquaintance among well-known characters," remarked

Joe Whitcomb, as he eyed the stranger dubiously. "What sort of a character is this one? Does he tell stories or drink rum? He looks as if he were capable of doing both."

Unconsciously and carelessly the young provincial had uttered a solemn truth. During the period which had elapsed since Dolly's emancipation from maternal restraint he had formed the acquaintance of an enormous number of men of the sort usually described as "great characters" or "odd geniuses," and of whom there is always a plentiful supply along upper Broadway, where they may be found on both sides of the street.

Many and various are the qualities and peculiarities that go to make up one of these "characters"; but no matter how eccentric or odd they may be, it has been noticed that there is one trait which they all possess in common, and that is a fondness for strong drink. It is for that reason, possibly, that they may be encountered in the greatest profusion and variety in saloons and cafés, and very seldom on church steps or at scientific lectures.

It often happens that a man becomes a legitimate and thoroughly well-authenticated "character" on the strength of some one happening or episode or experience in his life, by virtue of which he is entitled forever after to the consideration, esteem, and hospitality of his fellow-men. It was to this class of "characters" that the elderly man at the barren table belonged; and his claim to popular regard and the free cigars and drinks incident to it rested on the fact—recited many times a day between Twenty-third and Forty-second streets—that it was he who had put out the gas the last time that Edwin Forrest played. It was true that he had not been known to do a stroke of work of any description since the fateful night when it devolved upon him, as gasman of the theater, to extinguish the lights at the close of the last Forrest engagement; thus marking the end of the tragedian's career and the beginning of his own, for from that hour Broadway claimed him as a "great character."

Like others of his kind, the old-time gasman—nearly all of New York's "great characters," by the way, rejoice in the subsidiary title of "old-timer"—was ready for a drink, and was not averse to recounting, at considerable length, the circumstances under which he performed the melancholy duty which had transformed him from a simple mechanic into one of the recognized celebrities of the town.

Dolly paid for the bottle of champagne which the three drank, and would have ordered another had not Joe entered a strong protest, greatly to the disgust of the old-timer, who cheerfully announced his entire willingness to remain with his young friends for the rest of the afternoon.

"Great character, that," said Dolly, gaily, as the two friends found themselves once more on the sidewalk. But Joe Whitcomb made no reply. He was thinking rather sadly of the foolish course that his friend was pursuing, and trying to hit upon some plan to save him from the inevitable results of his folly.

A little later, as they were strolling up Broadway, a well-dressed, alert-looking man paused a moment in his walk to shake hands with Dolly and say to him, "Drop into the office this P. M. if you have time. I'm just back from Pittsburg, and I've got a message for you from a particular friend of yours."

"A message? What is it?" cried Dolly, excitedly. "Is she doing well there?"

"Doing well!" exclaimed Mr. Hustle — for it was he — "I tell you, my boy, that little girl is great, and the time is not far off when you'll have reason to be proud of the fact that you were the first one to start her in the theatrical business. Come around and I'll tell you all about it."

"Who's that?" asked Joe, as they walked along together.

"Oh, that's Mr. Hustle, one of the best-known theatrical managers in the city, and a particular friend of mine. By the way, I've an appointment with him this afternoon that I quite forgot about; so in a little while I'll ask you to excuse me for half an hour or so, and then I'll join you later."

"And who's that?" asked Joe again, as a man of striking appearance, with iron-gray hair, a long white mustache, and a handsome, impassive, clean-cut face, bowed and smiled with marked cordiality.

"That's—well, that's a well-known sporting man and bookmaker. I drop in and call on him once in a while. He's a thoroughbred sport, and square as a die."

Just at that moment the handsome, well-dressed man was saying to his companion, "I only wish the town was full of such fellows as that. He comes into my place once in a while and drops a few hundred."

"He looks to me like the sort of duck that 'ud play the wheel," rejoined the other, who had taken in Dolly's simple visage with one of the swift, searching glances I have already spoken of as peculiar to this part of the town.

"Those fellows always play the wheel; and what's more, we generally have the wheel ready for them in case they call," said the first speaker, significantly.

Our hero soon found a comfortable seat in a café in which to deposit his friend, and then made the best of his way to the office of Hustle & Hardup, where the senior member of the firm was awaiting him in a condition of nervous anxiety which he skilfully concealed under a mask of indifference.

"Hullo, Dillenbeck!" he cried cheerfully, as Dolly presented himself. "Come in here and shut the door behind you, so we won't be bothered. I thought maybe you'd like to read some of Miss Wheatleigh's notices and hear how she's getting along. Well, there are the Pittsburg papers; and she knocked 'em out the same way in Buffalo and Cleveland. Just listen to this: 'Miss Maude Wheatleigh, a young and extremely pretty actress, made a distinct hit in the comparatively unimportant rôle of *Polly Lightfoot*, which she played with a refinement, delicacy, and humor which completely captivated her audience, and at the close of the second act won her an enthusiastic call.' Here's another from the most conservative paper in western Pennsylvania: 'At the close of the second act a spontaneous call from all parts of the house brought *Polly Lightfoot* before the curtain. Miss Maude Wheatleigh, who sustains this rôle, is one of the most promising young actresses seen here in a long while. She is beautiful as well as clever, and many there were in the audience last night who predicted for her a brilliant future in her chosen calling.' Is n't that great for a lady who's been on the stage as short a time as she has? I tell you what it is; you 'll be surprised when you see her, she's improved so much."

"How soon did you say the company would be in New York?" demanded Dolly, who was fairly radiant with delight.

"New York!" gasped Mr. Hustle, horror-stricken at the suggestion. "You don't mean to tell me you want to nip that girl's career right in the bud by bringing her to New York now, do you? I would n't consent to it, and I doubt if she would, either. The part she has now is all very well for a young beginner — very nice ingénue part, and some very pretty lines in it I had Billy Freelance write in;—but if she comes before the New York public in it she'll be lost in the shuffle. No, sir, I've got great ideas of that girl's talents. Why, if I'm not very much mistaken, she is the coming actress of this country."

Mr. Hustle uttered these last words with a solemnity that made a deep impression on his hearer.

"The coming actress of this country," he murmured, in a sort of daze. "And how long will it be before she gets here, do you imagine? I mean, how long will it be before she will come out as a star?"

"That," replied Mr. Hustle, as he slapped his visitor on the back in the confidential, spine-stiffening fashion for which he was celebrated, "depends entirely upon the amount of nerve you've got. If you've got confidence enough in this lady's talent and beauty to back her in a starring tour my opinion is that within a very short time you'll not only have reason to be proud of your position as the man who discovered and brought her out, but you'll be making a barrel of money into the bargain."

For a few moments Dolly sat gazing into space and drumming with his fingers on the table. The proposition had come to him so suddenly that he needed time to collect his wits and think about it. Since he first embarked on the career which I have already indicated he had discovered that there was one crowning triumph in a wine-opener's life, and that was to be known as the man who was "putting up" for a popular actress. That very afternoon he had pointed out to Joe Whitcomb a long-eared young gentleman whose vacant face and self-conscious manner made him a target for the sharp glances of upper Broadway, and whose one glory was that he was spending five hundred dollars a month on a certain flashy, clever woman who belonged to one of the principal stock companies in the city, and had reached that time of life when women of her class feel the necessity of making hay before the final disappearance of the afternoon sun.

The callow, long-eared youth whose precious privilege it was to waste his patrimony on this hard-featured autumnal flower had been, but a few months before, a simple wine-opener like Dolly, and, like him, he was of city birth and training. Why is it that all the most distinguished of New York's gudgeons are born and brought up in the metropolis? The provinces seldom produce so fine a quality of fool as the variety that is nurtured in our own soil.

And now our hero realized that the opportunity to leap at one bound to the bright plane inhabited by the long-eared one and others of his kind had come to him unsought. In fancy he saw himself strolling into the St. Anthony café crowned with that matchless glory which can be won only by "putting up for an actress"; he saw the genials saluting him reverently; and it seemed to him that, as he made his progress through the throng, he left in his wake a phosphorescent chorus of "There goes Dolly Dillenbeck, the man that's putting up for Maude Wheatleigh."

It was a vision of bewildering, dazzling brilliancy that his fancy conjured up while he sat drumming with his finger-nails on Mr. Hustle's office-table — so dazzling, in fact, that he was afraid to seize the opportunity of realizing it without taking time for reflection.

## CHAPTER IX

On a dismal, rainy Sunday afternoon — it was the day after Dolly's interview with Mr. Hustle — Miss Pearl Livingstone, the principal actress of Messrs. Hustle & Hardup's traveling company, entertained a few of her fellow-artists in her room in the largest hotel of a great Western city, in which they had just finished their first week's engagement.

The floor was thickly strewn with the mutilated sheets of many-paged Sunday newspapers; for Miss Livingstone kept a voluminous scrap-book in which she pasted every favorable notice of herself that she was able to collect during her travels. Although an omnivorous buyer of newspapers, she never read anything but the dramatic department in each; and the speed with which she could find and clip from a forty-eight-page Sunday journal the three-line paragraph containing her own name had long been the theme of much admiring comment on the part of her professional associates.

These same associates, however, noticed with secret glee that the havoc made by Miss Livingstone's shears in the papers which lay scattered about the floor was not nearly as noticeable as it usually was on Sunday mornings in large Western cities, and that, moreover, two or three of the papers had not been cut at all. From one of these uncut sheets a large double-column portrait of Miss Maude Wheatleigh looked out upon them with a pleasant, self-confident smirk.

Miss Livingstone's guests, to the number of three, were seated at a round, bare table in the center of the room, engaged in a game of draw-poker with their hostess, who acted as banker, and at the same time dispensed occasional hospitality from a tall dark bottle containing the precious golden juice of the grain and bearing the label of a brand which enjoys in the highest degree the respect and confidence of the community.

Miss Wheatleigh sat directly opposite her hostess, by whom she was treated with a courtesy of the polished and elaborate sort that nothing less than intense feminine hatred and jealousy can prompt.

"Seen the papers this morning, Miss Livingstone?" inquired Mabel Morris, with a look of round-eyed innocence, as she shuffled the pack preparatory to dealing.

"I sent out for them, and I guess they're here somewhere, but I have n't had a chance to look at them.—It's your ante, I believe, Miss Temple."

"The only one I saw was the *Despatch*," continued Miss Morris, slyly kicking Miss Temple under the table as she dealt the cards, "and my! but there was a beautiful notice of Miss Wheatleigh, and a picture too.—You must have a mash on that reporter, Miss Wheatleigh. Can't you get him to say a word about the rest of us?"

"I don't think much of your dealing," cried Miss Livingstone, hastily, as she threw her cards on the table. "You can give me five more and I'll stay in, unless you're going to raise the price."

"What's the name of that *Despatch* critic, anyway?" inquired Miss Temple, carelessly, as she discarded two cards.

Her question was addressed to Miss Livingstone, who was believed to know the name, age, and personal characteristics of every dramatic critic and city editor in every town and city in the Union.

"Billy Fenwick is still there, I believe," she replied, "and he and I don't speak. —You've met him, I suppose, Miss Wheatleigh?"

"Never even heard of him before," rejoined Maude, calmly. "I 'm sure it was very nice of him, though, to put that notice in his paper. What sort of a man is he?"

"Like all other men—thinks that if a young girl is an actress she is necessarily destitute of self-respect. He tried it on with me once, and I just put him where he belonged. 'Mr. Fenwick,' I said to him, 'you seem to forget that you are addressing a lady who has forgotten more about etiquette than you ever knew in your life.'—I 'll take five cards.—'And as for the notices in your old paper, I would n't give a snap of my finger for them. I can get notices, and pictures too, in the biggest papers in this country. There 's nobody reads your old rag, anyway. I 'm sure I would n't buy a copy or be seen reading it—'"

"Where did that one come from that 's lying on the floor all crumpled up?" inquired Miss Morris, suddenly. And then

Miss Temple snickered, and the leading lady grew red in the face and nervously raised Miss Wheatleigh the limit, utterly forgetful of the fact that the heroine of this little romance had stood pat. After four raises back and forth Miss Livingstone called, and Maude displayed a king full on aces.

"Let's see what you've got!" cried Mabel, who in company with Kitty Temple had dropped out precipitately on seeing that Maude called for no cards on the draw.

Miss Livingstone threw her cards face down on the table without a word, and it was evident that she was very angry. If Mabel had seen the look on her flushed face it is probable that she would not have pushed the matter any further; but, eager to see what sort of a hand had impelled a player as cautious as the leading lady usually was to bet so recklessly against a pat hand, she seized the cards that the other had thrown down, and, turning them over, displayed a pair of jacks and a pair of threes.

"Leave those cards alone!" snapped the leading actress.

"Your hand belongs to the table," remarked Maude, who was thoroughly enjoying her triumph and the discomfiture of her opponent.

"I discarded an ace which bore a striking resemblance to one of those in your hand," exclaimed Miss Livingstone, in a voice that trembled in spite of her effort to charge it with a full note of icy, withering sarcasm.

"She stood pat," cried Miss Temple.

"Do you mean to intimate that I picked up one of your discards?" inquired Maude, speaking very quietly and looking her steadily in the face.

Just then there was a knock at the door, and a moment later Mr. Freelance entered. He saw at a glance that there was trouble afoot, and the jovial salutation died on his lips.

"I think I'll cash in," said Maude as she deftly stacked her chips into heaps of ten and pushed them across the table to the banker, who was now sobbing with rage and vexation. "If you'll be kind enough to control your emotions for a minute," continued Miss Wheatleigh, "you will find that you owe me just six dollars and a half."

Miss Livingstone buried her head in her hands and wept afresh, the others regarding her in silence.

Mr. Freelance withdrew with a smile of amusement on his face, making a sign to Maude to follow him.

"May I trouble you for the six-fifty?" asked Miss Wheatleigh.

The leading lady raised her head from the table and detached the amount from the little heap of bills and silver in front of her.

"There, take it, you nasty thing!" she cried. And as the winner carefully counted it and placed it in her pocket-book Miss Livingstone threw herself on the bed and gave way unreservedly to her grief.

Maude found Mr. Freelance waiting for her in the corridor. He laughed heartily at her description of the row at the poker-table, and astonished her by declaring that it was the most fortunate thing in the world that could have happened, so far as she—Maude—was concerned.

"How so?" she asked.

"Well, she's been very sore for some time because you've been getting so many good notices, and the sight of that picture in the *Despatch* and that column article in the *Recorder* was too much for her. I said as soon as I saw them that she'd be simply wild, and, to tell the truth, I went up to her room to see what sort of a mood she was in. I suppose that pot you raked in with your king full was merely the final unendurable straw. She's awfully close with her money, and I've no doubt that losing that big pot was a sore blow to her; but that was n't what she was mad about. It was because she's felt for a long time that you were becoming altogether too popular, and that your part had been built up so much that it was beginning to overshadow hers."

"It *has* been built up — thanks to you, Billy — and I think it *does* stick out a little more than it used to — thanks to me. As for the pictures and articles in the newspapers, I'm not quite vain enough to imagine that they are merely so many spontaneous tributes to my talent, and, to tell the truth, I've detected your fine Italian hand in one or two of them — that column in the *Recorder*, for instance. I'm ever so much obliged, Billy, and, believe me, I'll never forget it."

"Well, I've got something particular to say to you now," said Mr. Freelance, quietly ignoring her expression of gratitude, "and if you'll come into this chamber of desolation called the ladies' parlor, we'll sit down for a few minutes and talk about it. I've just had a long confidential letter from Hustle, who's got into a pretty tight place financially and sees only one road out of it—"

"And that road is through Mr. Dillenbeck's pocket-book, I suppose?" interjected Maude.

"Quite right; and an easy road it is to travel if you once get fairly started on it. Well, as you probably know, this show has been losing money lately, and if Hustle does n't send me something I won't be able to pay salaries on the first. They've pretty nearly talked young Dillenbeck into putting up a few thousands for a starring tour, and I guess you know whose name would be in big letters on the printing in that event. He must be easy fruit, that fellow, for I guess they've touched him pretty heavily already. About the only thing that stands in the way now is the contract with Livingstone; and I'm glad she's in the tantrums, because that makes it all the easier to egg her on to breaking it and throwing up her part. If they had consulted me they never would have signed with her, for I never had any faith in her drawing powers."

"She gets great notices in the papers, though," interrupted Miss Wheatleigh. "She's got a big scrap-book full of them."

"That's exactly the trouble. She's what I call a scrap-book actress. That book is her very staff of life. She gets all her engagements on it, and spends half her spare time in pasting clippings into it. She's got so many strong notices that I'll be hanged if I don't think the critics are afraid to say anything against her for fear they'd simply contradict what they said before. There are a whole lot of people in this business who get praised by all the newspapers and are never popular with the public. Livingstone is one of them."

"How do you account for the fact that an artist can please the critics, who certainly ought to be judges, and yet fail to please the public?" inquired Miss Wheatleigh.

"I'm not quite sure on that point myself," replied the business manager, thoughtfully, "but I rather think it's a case of the difference between the head and the heart. The playgoing public is a distinctly emotional body, that does n't take much trouble about the niceties of art. All it wants is to be moved in one way or another. It has a stomach that cries for emotional nutriment, just as a year-old baby has a stomach that cries for milk; and, like the baby, it neither knows nor cares for much of anything besides its own particular sort of food. The critic

"THE WINE CAME, AND CLOSE BEHIND IT LUMBERED JUDGE DOONOTHING."

is, as a general thing, a man of more than the ordinary degree of intelligence, and his brain is apt to be tickled by something new in the way of acting—something that's out of the common. It may be a touch of genius that interests him, or it may be merely some trick of gesture or intonation; but if it's different from what he's seen before, and particularly if it's altogether unlike what he expected to see when he came into the theater, the chances are that he'll write something favorable. As for Livingstone, she's been playing directly at the critics for years, and thinks very little of her audience."

"Did you ever notice the difference between her acting on a first night, when all the newspaper men are in front, and another plain, ordinary night, when there's nobody there but the audience?" interrupted Maude.

"There you have it in a nutshell: she does her best for the critics who fill her scrap-book, and she won't take any trouble for the people who buy their seats and from whom her salary comes. She thinks that it's the critics who give her the reputation, and Hustle & Hardup who pay her salary. She's away off in that belief, for it's the public that does both. Well, my dear, I've given you quite a little lecture on dramatic art, and it may be that it is all wrong — as far away from the truth as old Rungdown was when he taught you how to act. But to return to business. The question is, how can I induce Livingstone to break her contract?"

"If you don't pay her her salary for two or three months—" began Maude, but the other interrupted her.

"Then it would be Hustle & Hardup who broke the contract, and they'd never hear the end of it; for Livingstone's the most persistent litigant in the profession, and she'd take the case through every court in the country before she'd give in to them. It's a lucky thing you've understudied her part. I hope you're perfect in your lines, and I hope, too, that nobody in the company knows that you're up in them."

"Don't be afraid of me. I know them backward, and you can bet no one in the company ever saw me with the part in my hand."

"I guess I'll go and have a talk with her," said the business manager, after a moment of thoughtful silence on the part of both. "And in the mean time," he added, "keep out of her way and don't let her renew the quarrel."

## CHAPTER X

When Mr. Freelance was admitted to the room occupied by Miss Pearl Livingstone he found that the Sunday newspapers had been gathered up and arranged, neatly folded, in a heap on the table; that the bottle, glasses, cards, chips, and other implements of recreation and refreshment had disappeared; and that the leading lady had brushed her hair, put on a becoming wrapper, and seated herself in a rocking-chair with her back to the window, with a volume of poems in a showy binding and with richly gilded leaves in her hand.

The business manager knew at a glance that the actress was expecting a call from somebody, and he shrewdly surmised that

that somebody was himself. An association that covered a period of many years with Miss Livingstone had made him thoroughly familiar with all the artifices which she employed when dealing with her managers, as well as with the tricks and methods of her art. The wrapper, for example, was associated in his memory with many previous occasions when he had been obliged to call on her to settle some dispute with her managers, or to introduce some interviewing reporter or dramatic critic. He could hardly repress a broad smile when his eye fell upon the volume of poems with its gaudy binding and the gilding on the edges of its leaves. That and the scrap-book constituted Miss Livingstone's entire library, and whereas the last named was her almost constant companion, "The Garland of Gems" was never taken from the zinc trunk except when the actress desired to present herself to some visitor in a highly favorable light. Mr. Freelance had observed long before this that whenever his leading lady prepared herself to receive a call from a newspaper man she invariably disinterred the book of poetry, in order that the visitor might find her engaged in literary pursuits.

That the decorative volume of selected verse stood the actress in good stead is evidenced by the scrap-book, which contains innumerable references to it, of which the following, selected from a hundred of its kind, may be quoted as a fair example:

"Those who have only seen Miss Pearl Livingstone in her marvelous impersonation of *Beatrice, Countess Feathersham,* in 'Only a Perfect Lady,' doubtless think of her merely as the stately, polished, aristocratic woman who has been born and nurtured in the purple; a true noblewoman, haughty in carriage, calm and self-possessed in manners, and gracious to her inferiors despite her evident pride of birth. To those who have seen her only on the stage, the real Pearl Livingstone—the woman, not the artist—would prove a veritable revelation could they see her face to face in her own apartment, as she was seen by a *Bugle of Liberty* reporter yesterday afternoon.

"As the caller entered the spacious apartment in the American House which Mine Host Radcliffe has placed at Miss Livingstone's disposal during her engagement at the Opera House, a slender, graceful woman, with superb auburn hair and eyes of exquisite blue, rose from an easy-chair by the fire and came forward with outstretched hand and a welcoming smile on her lips—a vision of loveliest womanhood in a long shimmering robe of some soft, clinging fabric, well suited to her peculiar beauty.

"'You find me with my favorite companions,' said the little lady, with a smile of winning sweetness, as she bade her visitor be seated—'Browning, Byron, Tennyson, Longfellow. Ah, how I love them all! Do you know, my society friends in New York say that they would like to get into my library and burn up all my books, because they're so jealous of them. Just think of it! Burn up all my rare old folios and choice editions that I've devoted my life to collecting! Of course they are only in fun when they say that, but it really makes me shudder when I think of giving up the sweetest source of enjoyment that I have ever known, just for the sake of a few dinner-parties and balls and receptions that I really care very little about.'

"The book which Miss Livingstone laid aside when she rose to greet her visitor proved to be a richly bound volume of poems carefully selected from the works of the best English and American writers, and called appropriately 'The Garland of Gems.' This book is Miss Livingstone's constant companion on all her travels, and is a striking evidence of her refined literary taste."

A slight smile played over Mr. Freelance's face as his eye fell upon the familiar "Garland of Gems." He knew that she had determined upon some important move,—he was not sure what it was,—and he was glad, because he thought that if her anger and obstinacy and jealousy were sufficiently aroused to blind her to her own interests she might be induced to break her contract. At the same time he did not for a moment lose sight of the fact that he had in his leading lady a most difficult subject to handle—a professional litigant who preferred the court-room to the stage, because of the more generous facilities which it offers to an actress for the practice of her art; a woman who was thoroughly cognizant, also, of its claims on the popular attention as a fountain-spring of free advertising.

He knew, also, that whereas his opponent was only too glad of a chance to appear in tears and a tailor-made dress before a box full of sympathetic jurymen, his principals, Messrs. Hustle & Hardup, had both reached a period of life and a state of financial and other entanglements which rendered them averse to figuring in the fierce white light that shines upon the witness-box any more than was absolutely necessary. Unfortunately for his cause, Miss Livingstone was, as he well knew, fully alive to the peculiar conditions just mentioned, or, as either of the two might have put it, she knew she held a strong hand.

"To what fortunate occurrence am I indebted for the distinguished honor of this visit?" said Miss Livingstone, coldly, quoting from the second act of the society drama in which she had won so much renown. The line occurs in the scene in which *Sir Reginald Wheatcake* calls to offer her his hand in marriage, and is received with a degree of cold reserve such as is usually characterized in artistic circles as the "icy face."

"My dear Miss Livingstone," cried the business manager, "I came to tell you how sorry I am that you and Miss Wheatleigh have had this unfortunate misunderstanding. It's really too bad, because you both occupy such important positions in the company, and are together on the stage in so many scenes, that any coldness between you is sure to become apparent to the audience and mar the effect of the performance. Now if—"

"And why are we *both* important members of the company?" demanded Miss Livingstone. "I was engaged as leading lady by Mr. Hustle, and my position is distinctly stipulated in the contract. As you know perfectly well, other persons in the company have been pushed along and had their heads swelled with ridiculous notices and pictures in the papers until, I believe, they actually think they know how to act. I have put up with this and with other forms of impertinence for some time, Mr. Freelance, but I don't intend to any longer. It is not that I am afraid that my reputation as an artist will suffer by comparison with any of the amateurs who can only obtain an engagement through the good offices of wealthy young gentlemen who happen to take a fancy to them—not at all, Mr. Freelance. My standing in the profession is such that I am not at all uneasy; but I don't propose to be annoyed in this way any longer, and I warn you that you had better return to the old version of the play to-morrow night. I mean the original version that we played at the beginning of the season, before you undertook to *improve* it by building up every rotten part that could possibly interfere with those that were originally intended to carry the piece."

Miss Livingstone paused, partly to regain her breath, and partly because she had reached the end of the speech which she had carefully prepared in anticipation of the business manager's visit.

"There are so many people in the company who have wealthy friends," remarked Mr. Freelance, thoughtfully, "that I cannot imagine whom you refer to. As for the parts that have been built up, why, of course, I have endeavored to give some prominence to such artists as possess talents of the kind calculated to make them acceptable to the public; but I am sure that an actress of your experience and talent knows the artistic value of competent support. I cannot control the newspapers, and I will not be held responsible for the ravages of what you term the swelled head. It is a disease which is not even confined to the profession which you adorn."

"You need n't beat about the bush

with *me*, Billy," screamed the leading lady, excitedly. "You know I'm talking about that thing that calls herself Wheatleigh, and I tell you now she's got to be called down or else my understudy will read my lines on Monday night."

"What!" exclaimed the manager, with well-feigned horror and fear, "let Hardbrook go on in your rôle! You know as well as I do that she can scarcely play the part she's cast for now. I'd rather not raise my curtain at all."

"Very well, then," said the actress, decisively, for she thought she had him at a disadvantage, "we will play the original version to-morrow night. You can call a rehearsal in the morning if you like." And with these final words she resumed her perusal of "The Garland of Gems," while Mr. Freelance softly withdrew.

An hour later, while the leading emotional actress was pacing restlessly up and down her room, a hall-boy entered and handed her a note, addressed in the familiar handwriting of the manager. She opened it with nervous fingers, and then a broad smile of exultation swept over her face like a tidal wave, completely wiping out every trace of the anxiety, malevolence, and ill humor that had been portrayed there but a moment before.

Within the envelope was a brief call to rehearsal at eleven o'clock the next morning.

Many were the conjectures, busy the tongues, and incessant the whisperings, when the ladies and gentlemen of the company assembled on the stage of the opera-house the following morning, in obedience to the manager's call. The story of the quarrel in Miss Livingstone's room had been carried from lip to lip, and discussed in all its phases by every member of the company, not one of whom doubted for a moment that the leading lady had, as she usually did, asserted herself to the representative of Hustle & Hardup, and forced him to return to the original version of the play for the purpose of humiliating her rival. That she had gained her point surprised nobody; but how Miss Wheatleigh could smile and joke with so much naturalness under such circumstances was something that not one of them could comprehend. Either she held some trump card in reserve, or else she was a far better actress than she was supposed to be — and Maude's talents were generally recognized by her associates.

Even Miss Livingstone was disconcerted by the other's cheerful and unruffled demeanor, which not even her own supercilious tone could alter. Outside the lines demanded by the play the two ladies did not exchange a single word. Miss Hardbrook was not present. She was confined to her room with an attack of rheumatism, Mr. Freelance said, and it would be necessary to put some one else in her part that night—an easy matter, as she had very little to do. It was the leading lady who had chosen her for her understudy, and had carried her point with Hustle & Hardup. She had selected her because she knew there would not be the slightest chance of her making a hit in the rôle.

At a quarter before eight, while Miss Livingstone was in her dressing-room preparing to go on the stage, Mr. Freelance knocked at the door, and, on his plea that his business was urgent, was, after a brief delay, admitted to her presence.

"Here's a pretty state of things!" he exclaimed, handing her an open telegram. "We've got to play the new version, so you'd better make up your mind to it without any delay. Just read that despatch from Hustle."

"Do not change play as it now stands under any circumstances," was what the telegram said; and an expression of bitter wrath came into the face of the actress as she read it.

"I suppose this is some of your work," she hissed; "but I tell you now, as I told you last night, that I shall not go on unless the change is made. I don't care a snap of my finger for Mr. Hustle. Let him pay me the back salary he's owed me for the past two years if he wants me to act for him. No indeed, Mr. Billy Freelance, both you and Mr. Hustle ought to know by this time that I'm not a woman to be trifled with; and, what's more, I'd like to know what actress of my standing will go out under such a shaky management as his? It's me that draws the people into the house to pay the salaries, and if my name is out of the bill the business will drop, and don't you forget it."

The business manager's face had grown a trifle pale as he listened to this harangue, for he knew that the woman who sat before him in an old wrapper, hastily thrown on and buttoned about her neck, was an actress who could boast of a distinct following of her own. Her hair, hanging loosely down her back, was in the deft hands of her maid, who went on with her work with perfect unconcern. She was accustomed to disputes between her mistress and her manager, and as the former usually triumphed she continued to make her ready for the part which she had just refused, with passionate vehemence, to play. He knew also that the course which he was taking was a desperate one — that he was staking more than he could afford to lose on a single throw. It was not the first time in his life that he had taken such risks, and it had always happened that it was on account of some woman. One or two bitter memories came across him now as he looked down at the hard face with its ghastly make-up. For a moment he wished that he had not allowed himself to be drawn into the quarrel.

Then he thought of the other woman with the bright, laughing eyes, the smooth white skin, as yet unspoiled by greasepaint, the great talent that needed only a chance to assert itself, and the thought nerved him for what he had to do. Besides, he had gone too far to think of retreat.

"You see how it is," he said quietly; "I have nothing to do but obey orders. If you refuse to go on I shall have to do the best I can without you, or else keep the curtain down, and you know Miss Hardbrook is in no condition to play anything to-night. It would be cruelty to put her in such an exacting part as yours. I really think, my dear, that you had better reconsider your determination and—"

"Reconsider nothing!" exclaimed the actress. "If you play the new version you play it without me."

"Then," said the manager, calmly, "I am to understand that unless I disregard the explicit instructions of our managers—mine as well as yours—you will refuse to go on the stage to-night."

"Precisely," said Miss Livingstone, defiantly.

Mr. Freelance shrugged his shoulders and turned toward the door. Pausing on the threshold, he said: "Then I shall have to get along as well as I can without you. Shall I make the announcement before the curtain? It's almost time to ring up."

"By all means. I suppose, then, that I need not make up if I'm not going to play."

A few minutes later, the maid, who had been sent out on a reconnaissance, darted into the star dressing-room with the tidings that the business manager had stepped out at the prompt side and was addressing the audience. She had scarcely finished speaking when an outburst of applause brought an angry flush to Miss Livingstone's face.

"I'd like to know what those fools are making all that noise about!" she said, fretfully. "Is it because somebody else is going to play my part? Well, there won't be so much enthusiasm out in front when the same people go out and ask to have their money returned to them. The idea of that Hardbrook girl trying to play that part! Why, I don't think she even knows the lines!"

"If you please, ma'am," said the maid, in hesitating tones, "I don't think Miss Hardbrook is going to play it."

"She's not! Well, who will play it then, I'd like to know?"

"If you please, ma'am, I think Miss Wheatleigh is going to play it."

From that moment Miss Pearl Livingstone ceased to delineate emotional and hysterical rôles under the management of Messrs. Hustle & Hardup. And in after years those managers rose up and called

Mr. Billy Freelance blessed for the far-seeing astuteness which disposed of a litigious and troublesome star and gave to Miss Maude Wheatleigh a great opportunity.

# CHAPTER XI

PARTLY by reason of her own winning beauty and a resolute determination to make the most of her immature talents, and partly because of the diplomatic way in which her manager, in the few words which he spoke before the curtain, threw her upon the mercy of the audience as a young lady who had undertaken the difficult leading rôle at a moment's notice and without adequate preparation, Maude Wheatleigh achieved what might be termed a *succés d'éstime*. By that I mean that while her performance was not nearly as finished or effective as that of Miss Livingstone, who, as her associates always said, "knew her business," it was not so devoid of interest and color as to be described as an "artistic success" in the journals of the following day. Her impersonation of the chief part won for her a great deal of hearty applause, and no end of friendly notices in the local newspapers, and the unusual tribute of a special paragraph sent by wire to the principal newspapers in New York, where it was read with deep interest by the various people concerned in this story.

Mr. Hustle's eyes flashed with delight when his glance fell upon it, and he lost no time in showing it to Dolly, who was tremendously impressed with its importance as a tribute to the beauty and genius of the young actress who had come to fill so many of his waking thoughts.

"Just read that!" cried the wily Hustle. "I tell you, in all my experience as a manager I never heard of the Associated Press sending out a despatch about a lady who's been on the stage as short a time as this one has. And see how strong they've put it, too: 'The talented and beautiful young actress who pluckily assumed the rôle at a moment's notice, and achieved an immediate and unmistakable success with a large and critical audience!' Why, that little lady is n't much more than an amateur so far as experience goes, and yet here she is playing a heavy emotional part and making a big hit in it even if she does follow Livingstone, who, in my opinion, is the very best woman in her line in the whole country."

"It *does* look as if she had caught on," remarked Dolly, whose face was beaming with delight at the thought of the rays of reflected glory that would shine upon him as the young man of sportive tastes and generous tendencies who had been the very first to discover and place on the road to fame this fascinating young girl, whose beauty and genius were already beginning to attract the notice of both press and public.

Mr. Hustle must have divined his thoughts, for he slapped him confidentially on the shoulder, and exclaimed, in the convincing, enthusiastic tones which he could assume at any moment, even with bankruptcy staring him in the face: "My dear Mr. Dillenbeck, of all the young men that I know in this town you are, without exception, the most to be envied. How you, a comparatively young and inexperienced man, could have picked that girl for a winner the way you did is simply an everlasting source of wonder to me. Two years from now many a man in this town will be willing to give a good deal just to be able to say that he was the first one to give Maude Wheatleigh her start in life; and now, besides that, you've got a chance to make a pot of money out of your discovery, for the offer I made you on Saturday holds good. Don't forget that, my boy. We recognize that you have a certain moral claim on the proceeds of this young lady's genius, and I'm willing to talk business with you on the basis I mentioned the other day just as soon as you like."

Dolly's brain was teeming with bright pictures of future glory as he walked rapidly down Broadway after parting from Mr. Hustle. The young girl who had enlisted his interest such a short time before was certainly destined to become the footlight idol of the town, and then he would be known as her accepted admirer and discoverer. The more he thought about the splendid dignity of such a position in the eyes of the world, or of that portion of it in which he moved, the more eager was he to bite at the bait held out to him by the shrewd theatrical manager, and become the backer of her starring tour. Something seemed to be tugging at his purse-strings, which were never too securely tied; and before he had walked a dozen blocks he had about made up his mind to assume the risk of putting Miss Wheatleigh forward in a new play.

There *was* something pulling at his purse-strings at that very moment, for, unknown to him, Messrs. Hustle and Hardup were in close consultation as to the best method of bringing him to terms, while out in the western city Maude Wheatleigh was preparing, under the supervision and stimulus of Billy Freelance, who sat at her elbow, a long letter, couched in friendly, almost affectionate terms, telling the story of her triumph in the leading rôle, and artfully hinting at the great possibilities that lay before her provided she could obtain the financial support which was a necessary part of the equipment of every young actress, no matter how clever and beautiful she might be.

"Don't forget to inclose the clippings," said Mr. Freelance, looking over her shoulder as she signed her name. There were fully half a dozen of them, all complimentary in the highest degree; and in one of them her acting was said to be decidedly better than that of the woman whose place she had taken.

"I'll bet Livingstone was mad when she read that one," observed the manager as he stuffed the pieces of paper into the envelope. "She positively glared like a wild beast when you took your curtain-call at the end of the second act. Well, she broke the contract herself, so kicking won't do her any good. I can tell you one thing, my dear: I've taken big chances trying to put you ahead, and if I had it to do over again I'll be hanged if I would n't act differently."

"You've been so good to me, Billy!" cried Maude, impulsively; and then she took Billy's hand, which was resting on the table, in both of hers, bent her head until her forehead rested upon it, and said, in low, broken tones, "I owe everything to you; I can never repay you for what you have done for me."

"You read that line very well," said the manager, carelessly. "I must try to write it into one of your scenes."

Unconsciously she had used the very words which, at the other's dictation, she had just embodied in her letter to Dillenbeck; and now her face flushed with mortification as Mr. Freelance withdrew his hand and began to talk about the business of the tour. It was as if some fine bit of acting with which she had confidently expected to move her audience had been ruined by her own carelessness and stupidity.

"I think," said Mr. Freelance, presently, "that if Hustle succeeds in inducing your friend and admirer to advance money enough to float you on a starring tour, we had better cancel our dates and bring this great aggregation of talent back to New York, there to begin preparations at once for your début as a star. We're sure to lose money now that Livingstone is out of the cast, and you run the risk of becoming known as an actress who can't draw, long before you have a fair chance to show what you can do."

After saying this the business manager withdrew, leaving Miss Wheatleigh in a condition of mortification and self-abasement from which she did not recover for a long while. It was not often that he showed any resentment, for he was singularly even-tempered and good-natured; but when he did he seemed to have the faculty of saying precisely the things that would redden her face with annoyance, and at the same time not offer her the least excuse for a sharp retort. To tell her, in the very moment of her triumph, that if she played the leading part the company would go to pieces! Of what use were favorable newspaper criticisms if they did not draw audiences? It was brutal of him to say such a thing; all the more so because she knew it to be the truth. And then to mention Dillenbeck in the way that he did!—her friend and admirer! That was another and a far more bitter truth. It was he who had started her in the career that now seemed to promise so much. He had started her, too, with cold, hard money, as every member of the company knew, and it seemed to her that the taste of the bread of dependency was forever in her mouth.

She rose from the chair in which she had sat during her talk with her manager, and walked over to the window which looked out over the roofs and steeples and high chimneys of the bustling, active, progressive Western town. Her thoughts went back to the old days in Millbridge, and she wondered why it was that the little old house, with its cool dooryard, where the sunlight flickered down through the leaves of the maple-trees to the grassy turf, had not seemed to her as restful and beautiful then as it did now. She remembered how her father used to wander off into the woods to listen to the birds, and how her mother used to fume and fret because he was idling away his time instead of busying himself with the many "jobs" of sign-painting that seemed to be forever awaiting his brush.

"If poor papa had been blessed with a little of the vim and push and effrontery and cheek and recklessness that have built this city up from nothing in a few years, he would have worked at masterpieces instead of jobs," she said to herself; and then a smile of merriment swept across her face as she thought of Mrs. Dillenbeck and her anxiety about her son.

"I only hope," said Maude to herself, "that that woman can look down from her heavenly abode and see what her promising young son is doing with the money that his father made and she saved for him. Buying drinks for every loafer that will flatter him, and putting up for an actress! Yes, and that actress the poor little sewing-girl whom she wanted to drive out of Maplefield. I wonder if Dolly ever knew why his mother carried him off so suddenly that summer. And is n't it queer he never found out where I came from? The truth is, he 's so busy thinking about himself that he does n't really care anything about other people. Well, I hope his mother can look down and see him putting up his money to back an actress!"

The remembrance of the fact that a young man was "putting up" for her, as her professional associates termed it, came over her again with annoying persistency. She tried to divert her thoughts into some other channel, and again she stood in fancy beside the bench in the old shop, and heard her father talking to her in low, quiet tones while he worked. It was from him that she had inherited the talent, genius, power,—whatever it might be,—that had enabled her to move that great houseful of people the night before. Even now the applause seemed to be ringing in her ears. She remembered him now with a tenderer regard than ever before.

After all, why should not one inherit an artistic temperament from a house- and sign-painter? I once knew a bankrupt who possessed the very finest literary taste, and who had been, prior to his bankruptcy, a book-publisher.

## CHAPTER XII

THERE came a day when Dolly Dillenbeck entered the St. Anthony café with a look of exultation on his face which was precisely in keeping with his gorgeous fur-lined overcoat; and that garment would have made him a marked man in any community in which straights and flushes enjoy the standing that rightfully belongs to them.

In homely expressive phrase it might have been said of Dolly, that afternoon, that he "felt his oats." So noticeable, indeed, was the look of complacency and importance that lit up his round, simple face that Judge Doonothing, Mr. Rungdown, and two other well-known genials rose as he entered, and came forward, each from a different corner of the café, to shake hands with him. At Dolly's invitation they marched up to the bar with the promptness and precision of a file of veterans, and, when the glasses were filled, instinctively turned their faces toward the gilded youth, as if they expected some word or sign explanatory of his exultant mood. They were not disappointed.

"Gentlemen," said Dolly as he raised his wine-glass, "I want you to drink to the success of a certain young lady who is well known to one of you at least" (Mr. Rungdown bowed with suitable humility), "and who will before long be known to you all as an actress of beauty and talent; for I hope that you will all be present at her début as a star in about six weeks. Meantime we will wish her health, happiness, and prosperity."

In this manner our hero made known to a select circle of his intimates the outcome of an ardently cherished plan which had already cost him innumerable anxious vigils and long consultations with Miss Wheatleigh, Mr. Hustle, and Mr. Freelance, to say nothing of various cash advances and guaranties to the extent of several thousand dollars.

It had been finally settled that Miss Wheatleigh should make her appearance as the star of a new play under the management of Messrs. Hustle & Hardup, and it had also been determined that Mr. Freelance should be retained to devote himself exclusively to her interests. This was done at the special request of the young actress, who had already formed a high estimate of his abilities, and with the full approval of the managers, both of whom had complete confidence in his discretion, sound judgment, and unswerving fidelity to those who employed him. And never in the course of his career had Billy Freelance gone into any enterprise with half the enthusiasm and keenness that he displayed now in the interest of the girl whose talent he had been the first to notice. For it was he who had the right to pose as the "discoverer" of Maude Wheatleigh, as Dolly had felt only a personal interest in her, and, to do him justice, a generous desire to help a friendless girl along, while Mr. Hustle's only thought when he engaged her had been to secure the thousand dollars of which he stood in sore need.

"New York! Not for months yet!" had been Billy's rejoinder when Dillenbeck asked him how soon the young débutante would appear on the boards of a metropolitan theater. "New York is a dangerous place for a new actress. Let her learn her profession in the smaller towns, where we may be able to persuade them that she's really acting and not making believe, and then, when she feels sure of herself, and we feel sure of her, and of her play, too, it will be time enough to talk about New York. It's a great show town for a successful star, but a very bad one for a girl to fail in at the beginning of her career."

So it was settled that the New York appearance should be postponed indefinitely; but Mr. Freelance proposed as a compromise that Maude should enjoy the advantage of a "grand début" in some city not too far away, to which Dolly might journey with a party of friends in order to give her what he termed "a good send-off." At the same time Mr. Freelance stipulated that prior to this début she should be allowed to practise her new art on various small communities. In this way, Mr. Freelance informed his patron, she would not only gain experience, but he himself would have an opportunity to make such changes in the play as might be needed.

To this compromise Dolly was obliged to give a reluctant consent. He could see no glory in "backing" an actress who appeared only in provincial towns and cities and was absolutely unknown to those people in New York who alone knew what a wine-opener was and could appreciate the honors that rightly belonged to him when he reached the pinnacle on which dwell only the elect who "put up" for starring tours. But he determined to make up for his disappointment by making her début in Albany so brilliant and noteworthy an event that tidings of it would echo through the cafés of New York for many weeks afterward. His little head was full of this project when he entered the St. Anthony Hotel in the manner already described and acquainted his friends with his good fortune.

But the Dolly Dillenbeck who proudly marshaled his friends in front of the bar that bright winter's afternoon was not a circumstance in point of exultation and self-complacency to the gilded youth of similar facial aspect, and wearing the same fur-lined overcoat, who stood in the Grand Central Depot one bleak, windy morning, ushering his friends into the private car which was to bear them to Albany. Mr. Freelance was with him, for he too had invited some citizens of the sort likely to lend *éclat* to any ceremonial; and as he ran his eye over the two lists of expected guests he nodded his approval frequently and with emphasis.

"General Whiffletree is just the man for such a trip as this. I hope he 'll wear that military-looking cape-coat of his. He 'll make a great impression plowing round the lobby of the Delavan House with that on. You 've got Judge Doonothing here, of course. Make him wear those gold eye-glasses and talk loud in the bar-room. You see, these people are of no earthly use to any one except as a bluff, and they 're all great at that. I 'd rather have them along than the President of the United States and his cabinet, because they'll make more noise and do more talking. Senator Hardscrabble? That's the big windy stuff with the long chin-whiskers, is n't it? You have n't forgotten old Rungdown, I hope. He'd better sit in a box with three or four of the most impressive-looking of these genials and lead the applause. Dr. Puffe —he's all right; just give him all he wants to drink and he'll be good for no end of paragraphs in the Sunday papers, which is just what we bring him along for. I must see to it, by the way, that they all have canes or umbrellas."

"What for?" asked Dolly, innocently.

"What for!" rejoined Mr. Freelance. "Why, to applaud with, of course. I'm going to have them scattered all over the house, with instructions to keep their eyes on old Rungdown, and when he starts the applause they'll all chime in; then the aborigines will be sure to follow suit.

There's nothing like an occasional spontaneous burst of enthusiasm to make a first night go off well. Good gracious! you have n't gone and asked that infernal old ham, Skye Borders, have you?"

"Why, certainly I did," responded Dolly, who was growing a little restive under Mr. Freelance's frank comments on his closest friends. "And why should n't I? Is n't he well known both as an actor and a dramatist? Why, he's got a beautiful play already written that he'll let us have in case this one is a failure. Palmer wants it the worst way; and Daly wrote him only yesterday, begging him to come around and read it to him; and yet he won't go near them, just because he promised to let me have the first chance to produce it. Besides that, I've no doubt he'd consent to play a part in the piece himself, and he has the reputation of being one of the very best character-actors in the country."

Mr. Freelance patiently waited, with a look of pity on his face, until his patron had finished, and then said, "Yes, he's had that play for at least eleven years, and he gives it a new name every six months. He's read it to me twice already. Why doesn't he take it to Daly? It will be quite a treat for him to hear an author read a play. So if this piece of ours is a failure he'll let us have his, will he? Well, do you imagine that he's going to exert himself to boom *this* play when he's got one of his own to dispose of? Is he going to applaud our actors if he's dying to get an engagement himself? My dear boy, never bring a dramatist into a house on a first night. There's not one of those fellows who hasn't a play, and sometimes two, in his coat-tail pocket, ready to flash at you in case your own piece is a frost. And this man Borders is the worst of the lot, because, in addition to the crime of writing plays, he was once an actor—not much of an actor, but just enough to give him the right to sneer at all other actors. And, moreover, he is a morose, disappointed man, who was cut out for a grocery clerk, but got stage-struck at an early age, and has been ruined by it. There's not an artistic calling you can name that is n't overrun with such men as that, and the worst of it is that they never seem to understand that they fail because of their own utter incapacity, and not because the world is against them. Well, I'll have a talk with this fellow going up on the train. I guess I can fix him so that at least he won't do us any harm."

"Let me take a look at your list," said Dolly, suddenly. "Who's that man, Peter Proudfit? What did you ask him for?"

"Because he wears a broadcloth suit and has long white chin-whiskers. He'll make as good a showing as General Whiffletree, although he has n't a military title. Then there's little Habenichts—

he'll register himself Baron von Habenichts; and there's Major Rafferty—I asked him because he's an Irishman; and so it goes. There's not a man there that won't be of some use to us. They're just the right sort; but don't lend one of them a dollar or you'll never see it again. There comes the General, and two or three more genials after him."

As the train steamed out of the depot our hero, always mindful of the great rôle he had chosen to play through life, summoned one of the colored attendants of the special car, and bade him open half a dozen quarts without delay; and five minutes later his guests were quaffing his wine and sounding the praises of the perfect gentleman and nature's nobleman whose privilege it was to be their host, for all the world as if they were seated about a table in the St. Anthony House. The trip to Albany was one prolonged carnival of wine-opening, varied with an occasional distribution of twenty-five-cent cigars; and by the time the train had reached its destination every member of the company not only admitted, but declared with vociferous ostentation, that the whole world did not contain a more polished, scholarly, whole-souled, and large-hearted gentleman than T. Adolphus Dillenbeck, now known to that contemporaneous Fame which gilds a few of the brows between the Fifth Avenue Hotel and the Casino as " wine-opening Dolly, the Pride of Upper Broadway."

As the train crossed the Hudson from East Albany, Dolly, seated in pensive mood beside the car-window, which the colored porter had considerately opened, saw the great white shining dome of the capitol before him, and in his fevered fancy pictured himself a prince entering his own realm in splendid triumph, there to be anointed with the divine oil. It was scarcely three years since he first came on the turf, and here he was, the acknowledged prince of wine-openers, riding in a private car at the head of as brave a company of genials—courtiers they would have been termed in the olden time—as ever followed in a monarch's train. Moreover, was he not already crowned with that bright diadem which marks the supreme development of the wine-opener—the diadem which decks no brow save that of him who "puts up" for an actress?

The train rolled slowly into the Albany depot, and Dolly reflected with just pride that he had opened four cases of champagne since they left New York.

They all trooped across the street to the hotel,—Dolly was sorry it was not half a mile away, so that they could have driven there in carriages,—and when Mr. Freelance had registered the names of the party, titles and all, there was no gainsaying the fact that the list was one calculated to make a profound impression on any one who saw it.

Unlike the others, Billy Freelance had not been idle on the way up from the city. He had arranged with Mr. Rungdown to take charge of the claque, and had given him a list of cues for laughter and applause. Besides that, he had taken Mr. Borders aside—just as he was beginning to croak ominously about failure—and impressed upon him the fact that if the play were to fail that night Mr. Dillenbeck would be frightened out of the business, and refuse to advance another cent; while, on the other hand, if it were to prove a tremendous success, he would feel encouraged to go ahead and branch out. "I'm not satisfied with the play we've got now, I can tell you that," Mr. Freelance had observed, with refreshing frankness, "and if we make any sort of a success with it I shall insist upon getting another one; but it's no easy matter to get a good piece, especially when you're dealing with a man as suspicious as Mr. Dillenbeck. There's only one way to stand in with him, and that is to manifest the greatest enthusiasm for every scheme he gets up, and pretend you think his play and his star and the theater and the company, and everything else connected with it, are the very best in the market. If a man makes any sort of criticism,—and there are men here right in this car who would n't hesitate to repeat it to him with additions of their own,—then he gets suspicious right away, and says to himself, 'That man is jealous,' whereas he might be the truest and most disinterested friend he had in the world."

From that moment the company could show no finer specimen of open-hearted geniality and enthusiasm than the usually saturnine and vindictive playwright, Mr. Skye Borders.

At precisely eight o'clock that evening

Maude Wheatleigh, dressed for the first act, stood on the stage of the theater looking through the peep-hole in the curtain, and listening to Billy Freelance's description of the journey from New York.

"Why in the world does that silly fellow surround himself with such people?" demanded Maude, suddenly, turning her face from the peep-hole and addressing the business manager. "He brought that pompous old Whiffletree up to see me some time ago, and of course I had to be polite to him; but of all stupid, conceited, whisky-drinking bores, he is about the worst I've ever met. Has n't Mr. Dillenbeck any nice friends of his own age, or any age, for that matter, that he must always be running around with those wearisome old codgers who make him buy wine for them and, I've no doubt, get lots of money out of him?"

"My dear," replied the talented factotum of the firm of Hustle & Hardup, "that young man's strongest passion is his vanity; and so long as those senators and judges and generals and majors continue to feed it, just so long will he lend them money and pay for whatever they want to eat and drink. That crowd has cost him thousands and thousands of dollars already, and I rather think he'll get tired of the game before they do. I suppose you know why he went into this theatrical venture?"

"I suppose," replied the girl, steadily, but with a slight color creeping out beyond the limit of the rouge and greasepaint that stained her cheeks—"I suppose it was in order to have those barroom loafers nudge him in the ribs, and grin and wink and crack their clumsy jokes about the 'little actress he's backing.' Oh yes, I know well enough the sort of figure he'll cut in the St. Anthony House, and I hope his *vanity* will be gratified, because I can tell you he won't get anything else out of it. I suppose I ought to be grateful because he's given me a chance I would n't have had otherwise, and so I am, for that matter; but my gratitude does n't blind me to his real motives. I know something about the world and the men in it, Mr. Freelance, even if I have been only a short time 'on the turf,' as you call it."

She turned away abruptly as she finished speaking, and applied her eye once more to the hole in the curtain.

"You know that scene you have with Tommy toward the close of the third act?" remarked Mr. Freelance, after a moment's pause.

"I ought to; I 've rehearsed it often enough," she answered shortly, without turning her face.

"Well," continued Billy, "you want to read those lines exactly as you 've been talking to me just now."

"There they come!" she exclaimed,

making no sign that she had heard him; "there comes that big fat Judge Doonothing—I can tell him from your description; and there's a real nice-looking old gentleman with a long white beard—"

"I brought him along just on account of that white beard," remarked Billy, dryly.

"And there's that tiresome old Rungdown! I suppose if I ever make a success he'll go around telling everybody that he taught me all I ever knew about acting. Well, I'm happy to say—and it's thanks to you, my dear boy—that some of the things he took so much trouble to teach me about the 'histrionic art,' as he calls it, I *don't* know now, because I've taken particular pains to forget them. But what on earth did you bring him up here for, Billy?"

"What for! Why, he's one of the distinguished guests, and a very important one, too, because he's going to lead the applause. He's got his list of cues the same as the leader of the orchestra has, and when he applauds, Judge Doonothing, old man Whiffletree, and all the rest of them will follow suit. Each one is provided with a cane or an umbrella. Then to-morrow you'll have the pleasure of reading about the spontaneous outbursts of enthusiasm which showed plainly what a deep impression the young actress had made on the refined and critical Albany public. But you'll notice this evening that all the spontaneous enthusiasm will start right from that right-hand upper box."

To his complete surprise Maude Wheatleigh turned upon him with cheeks that were now fairly ablaze, and exclaimed, "Do you people who traffic in art and genius ever think how you degrade everything that you touch? I don't believe you do, or you would have been ashamed to say to me what you did just now. For months I have been devoting every atom of talent I possess to this part. I've literally lived in it, and I shall cry to-night when I come to one or two scenes in it. I don't know whether I'll be able to *read all the lines*, as you say. All I care for is to make the people laugh and cry with me. That's what I've been living for and working for all this time, and now you come to me just before the curtain goes up, and tell me you've brought up a carload of bar-room loafers from New York,—men who never knew an honest emotion in their lives,—and *they* are to let the people know when to applaud and when to weep. I tell you it's outrageous, and especially from *you*."

She paused a moment after this outburst, and then went on with forced calmness: "Have n't you told me from the very first that you had faith in me? How much faith have you in my ability when you bring a horde of men on from

New York, and give them canes and umbrellas, that they may teach the people when to applaud and when to cry? Never mind, though; there will be some applause to-night that will not begin in that right-hand upper box. It will come from the left side."

She laid her hand over her heart as she said this, and it seemed to him that her voice broke a little at the last. She was looking through the peep-hole again now, and before he could frame a reply to her indignant words she said, "There's Mr. Dillenbeck, and I do believe he's coming back on the stage. I told him I could n't bear the sight of you, and only tolerated you for business reasons."

"Then you'd better go into your dressing-room," replied Billy; "anyway, it's pretty near time to ring up."

# CHAPTER XIII

THANKS to Mr. Freelance's success in awakening interest in his star by means of crafty newspaper paragraphs and a liberal distribution of photographs, not to mention a judicious scattering of free tickets, the theater was filled with what the newspapers described as a "large and thoroughly representative audience" on the occasion of Miss Wheatleigh's début. In the upper right-hand box sat the most impressive-looking of Dolly's invited guests, under the guidance of Mr. Rungdown, who also had command of the forces on the floor below and those in the balcony directly opposite. General Whiffletree, Senator Hardscrabble, Judge Doonothing, and the elderly gentleman with the long white beard were the other occupants of the box. Mr. Hustle sat with a detachment of genials in orchestra chairs, while Dolly roamed in and out of the theater, and from the stage to the auditorium, too much excited to sit still in one place a single minute.

The first act went well—at least that is what everybody told our hero when they followed him from the theater to a nearby place of refreshment, in order that they might once more drink to the success of the débutante; but to Mr. Freelance it seemed that Maude was not quite at her best, and he took pains to go back to her dressing-room and ask her, in penitent tones, if there were anything he could do for her, and whether she had forgiven him for trying in his blind, brutal way to make her début an exciting and noteworthy success.

"Yes, Billy," said the girl, turning to him with a powder-puff in her hand, "you're forgiven; but I do wish you had n't told me about those old guys in the box. I could n't help looking there every minute or two to see whether Rungdown was getting ready to applaud or not, and once I saw him pull out his handkerchief and draw it across his eyes like this, and then the rest of them followed suit like a company of soldiers. But, Billy, you must lend that third man in the row one of your white handkerchiefs, because he's got nothing but a red bandana, and it does n't match the box curtains. However, perhaps there 'll be some applause in the next act that won't start from that box." And something in the tone of her voice, in her firm, resolute mouth, convinced him that the débutante was very much in earnest that night.

The play was one of the class, common enough nowadays, dealing with the period of our Civil War; and Maude was the young girl of humble circumstances whose lover, having quarreled with his father on her account, had gone to the front, after a brief pause to enable him to put on his uniform in order that he might say goodby to his sweetheart, while the regimental band played "The girl I left behind me" and the glittering bayonets of the departing troops could be seen through the front windows of the drawing-room, in which all the characters in the play were assembled.

All this and a great deal more happened in the first act; and in the second, which was universally admitted by the visiting genials to be superior to the first, the exciting scenes of army life, in camp and in the rifle-pits under the guns of a gloomy-looking fortress, were depicted, with a moderate degree of accuracy and a liberal use of red fire and smoke. In this act Maude appeared as a hospital nurse in the most becoming of costumes, ostensibly engaged in ministering to the sick and wounded, but in reality looking for her lover, whom she found at last ill with a fever and burning with a desire to go to the front and distinguish himself.

The scene of the third act was laid in New York, where the lover's father had been engaged in speculations on the gold market and had amassed a vast fortune, which had served to make him more purse-proud than ever, and to strengthen his resolve to have nothing to do with the ungrateful son who had not only refused to give up the girl of his choice but had also insisted upon going out to fight his country's battles when he might have stayed at home and made a fortune in Wall Street.

During this act the heroine arrived from the field, determined to effect a reconciliation between the father and son at all costs, even if it were necessary for her to give up all claim on her lover and release him from his vows. She entered the rich speculator's drawing-room just as he was in the midst of a discussion with his wife in regard to the conduct of their son, whom he denounced as a worthless, ungrateful dog who deserved to be a pauper for the rest of his days for neglecting opportunities to get rich such as present themselves but once in a generation. And then he turned to the state of the gold market, crying exultantly, "All I want to see is another big battle that will come pretty near wiping out our army, and then gold 'll go kiting up into the hundreds and I 'll be able to retire."

Then his wife, horror-stricken at his words, reminded him of their boy who was somewhere at the front fighting for the old flag; and just at this moment Maude entered, threw aside her waterproof cloak, and besought the father to write a letter of forgiveness to his son imploring him in his mother's name to return at once to New York. She told him how bitterly the boy had felt his parents' displeasure, and how he was now sick with the fever but still keeping in the ranks in order that he might take part in the very next battle. There had been some cases of shamming in his regiment, and he would run no risk of being classed with the cowards.

And while she was pleading passionately with the hard, money-getting father, hoarse cries arose in the street outside, and grew louder and louder every moment. The mother knew at once the meaning of those cries, as what mother did not in those days? The newsboys were shouting extras, there had been another battle, and her boy was at the front!

"Another battle!" cried the father, excitedly. "Then that means another victory for Johnny Reb, and to-morrow gold will touch the two-hundred mark."

"Our boy at the front, and you stand there talking about the gold market!"

"I DON'T CARE A SNAP OF MY FINGER FOR MR. HUSTLE."

cried his wife, reproachfully. And then the newsboys came thundering down the street, the door was thrown open, and, followed by a gust of snowflakes, a boy rushed in with his roll of papers under his arm, threw one down on the table, and exclaimed, "Big fight at Lookout Mountain!"

"Lookout Mountain!—that's where our boy is!" cried the mother, sinking back into her chair, her face white with anxiety.

"Yes, he's there, and I know that he was in that fight," said Maude, in steady accents, advancing to the father, who seemed to suddenly realize that his only son was in danger. "Perhaps," continued the young girl, in tones that made their way to every heart in the audience—"perhaps he is lying dead before the big guns under the shadow of the fort; but read what the paper says."

The silence in the house was broken

only by the crisp rustling of the paper as the old man unfolded it and tried to read. Suddenly he let it fall to the floor and sank into a chair. "There it is," he said—"there's his name in the list; but I can't read any more. You read it, girl, if you can."

"I can read it," said Maude, calmly, as she advanced to the footlights with the paper in her hand.

There was a moment of what is called "dramatic suspense" as she ran her eye down the column; then she turned to the father and mother, and read, in clear, ringing tones, in which there was a distinct note of triumph: "'Thomas Wheelwright promoted for bravery on the field of battle.' There, what do you think of the gold market now?"

It may have been because of the memories which the scene awakened in the hearts of those who were alive at the time when extras were cried at midnight in the streets, or it may have been because of the rare, sympathetic quality in the young girl's voice; but certain it is that she stirred her hearers to their very hearts' cores, and the curtain went down on such a storm of applause as it falls to the lot of but few artists to listen to. Even the distinguished visitors in the upper right-hand box were visibly affected, and forgot to watch their chief of claque. General Whiffletree sniffed audibly, and wiped his eyes with his large and impressive bandana handkerchief. The scene brought back its memories to him, for, to tell the truth, he had never been south of Mason and Dixon's line until he joined the horde of invading carpet-baggers after the war; and the midnight cries of newsboys selling extras had been a familiar sound in his ears during those stirring times when they were of such frequent occurrence.

"I tell you, gentlemen," he said, with the air of one who is in the habit of settling vexed questions with a single word, "that girl is great; and my young friend, Dolly Dillenbeck, may thank his stars that he came to me for advice when he first thought of putting her on the stage." And the General stalked off in search of his young patron, with the rest of the genials at his heels.

Billy Freelance was the first to congratulate the young star on her splendid triumph, for it had proved a far greater triumph than any one had anticipated. He found her seated in her dressing-room, panting, with flushed cheeks and sparkling eyes. She looked up at him as he entered, and smiled triumphantly, but, it seemed to him, with a wonderful sweetness. "Well," she said, "did *that* applause begin in the right-hand upper box? Hark! they're beginning again; yes, that's another curtain-call, and it's from the people, too. Your distinguished guests from New York are not making all that noise. They're probably all of them in a corner bar-room by this time, guzzling whisky as if that were the best thing life could offer them."

"Another call, Miss Wheatleigh!" exclaimed the stage-manager, putting his head in at the door. And the young girl tripped out of the room, stood for a moment in the entrance while the curtain was drawn aside, and then went out before the footlights and bowed gently, with a deprecatory look and gesture, to the most enthusiastic demonstration ever known in the theater. She smiled again as she passed the business manager on her way back to her dressing-room. "That upper right-hand box is empty," she said, quietly. "You ought to have tied your distinguished guests to their chairs, so that they would n't quit work before the whistle blew." And without waiting for him to reply to her sarcasm, she went into her dressing-room to get ready for the last act.

## CHAPTER XIV

In a large room which formed an exact cube, and was furnished exactly like forty thousand other rooms of similar size and shape which are devoted to the use of travelers throughout the United States, Maude Wheatleigh sat up in bed the morning after her début, and for the first time in her life drank from the cup of fame until she was satiated. In other words, she read the criticisms of her performance in the morning papers until puffery began to pall upon her. Then she rang for her breakfast.

In the golden centuries of which the poets have sung,—and sung, too, far more tunefully than the poets of to-day are singing,—the laurel wreath was the accepted symbol of fame, and was used to deck the brow of poet, warrior, king, or statesman. It is even used at the present day for that purpose by sculptors and painters, although the actual wreath is no longer employed.

Now if I were an artist with a turn for modern realism I would portray my hero, not in an impossible cloak, not standing beside a marble column with a roll of manuscript in his hand, not decked with a crown of laurel—I would represent him in a modern hotel room, sitting up in bed and reading about himself in the morning newspapers, and looking critically at double-column portraits of himself —process reproductions of photographs given out by his business manager or advertising agent the day before. And I would endeavor to catch the expression of his face at that supreme moment when his greedy eye devours the half-column of eulogy which makes him feel that there are, after all, some people in the world who have the right appreciation of true greatness.

Therefore I have so contrived this story as to afford my readers a brief glance at my heroine at one of the most interesting and picturesque points of her career, and I hope that no one will complain because the glimpse thus offered is taken in the privacy of her own room, where she is drinking in those deep drafts of newspaper flattery which play such an important part in a theatrical career.

Of course Maude had been puffed a great many times, and sometimes at great length and effectively, since her first appearance on the stage; but now, as she sat with the papers before her and her mind and heart filled with memories of last night's triumph, it seemed to her that she had leaped at one bound into the public eye, and that her path thereafter would be an easy one beneath her feet. One critic described her as "a combination of Adelaide Neilson and Sarah Bernhardt"; a second called her "the American Duse"; and a third observed that no managers had ever paid a higher compliment to the critical and refined Albany public than Messrs. Hustle & Hardup had in choosing that city as a suitable place for Miss Wheatleigh's début.

"Well, I suppose I am famous at last," said Maude to herself as she rested her chin on her hands and gazed thoughtfully out of the window at the big patch of blue sky which she could see above the roof of the house over the way. And then her thoughts went back, as they did at every moment of triumph or adversity in her life, to the old gray farm-house in Millbridge, with its brown path leading to the well, the kitchen where her mother was at work, and the dim forest where she used to wander with her father, listening to the birds and watching the rabbits that crossed their path.

"I owe a good deal to poor papa," she said to herself, "and to mamma too," she added as an afterthought; "and I suppose I owe a good deal to that old Mrs. Dillenbeck, for if it had n't been for her terrible anxiety about that precious boy of hers I 'm sure I never would have even remembered him. What a lucky accident it was, meeting him the very minute I touched the New York pavement! And as for Billy—"

But at this moment the servant entered with the breakfast tray, and the young actress postponed her meditations until some more convenient moment.

Tidings of Maude Wheatleigh's extraordinary success were carried to New York by Mr. Hustle and the band of invited guests, whom nobody believed, and were subsequently confirmed from more reliable sources. Before a week had elapsed a New York manager went on to Syracuse, where the company was performing, and at the close of the play sought out Mr. Freelance and proposed that he should bring the new star to New York without delay, and ended by offering them very advantageous terms at his own theater. Dolly, who had been with the company ever since the auspicious début in Albany, was for closing with him at once, and would have done so had it not been for his business manager, who declared that to go to New York at that time would be simply to court disaster. "You see how much this girl has improved in the short time she's been before the public," he reasoned; "well, give her a chance and she'll go on improving, so that by next season she'll stand some show with a Broadway audience. There'll be more interest in her then, too, because of course I'll keep her name in the papers as much as possible, and people will *want* to see her then.

They have n't heard of her yet, and we 'd have to create an interest while she was playing. If she were to fail there this spring—and I tell you plainly I don't feel sure of her yet, or of the play either—it would be very hard to get time for her next fall or winter, and even if she did she would n't be a novelty then. Let us go on as we are for the rest of this season, playing the smaller cities and giving her a chance to study and to practise her art on the yokels."

But Dolly was too much elated over his star's success to listen to the counsel of his experienced and sagacious manager, and he would have acceded to the New-Yorker's terms if Mr. Freelance had not as a last resource appealed to the actress herself and convinced her of the folly of venturing on a metropolitan engagement at the fag-end of the season.

Maude Wheatleigh's career had been so remarkable, and her success so quickly and easily achieved, that Mr. Freelance, although usually anything but a sanguine man where adolescent genius was concerned, was prepared for almost any extraordinary turn of affairs; but when he found that she indorsed his views on the question of a New York engagement, and declared that it would be far better to wait six months at least, he literally fell back in his chair, stupefied by her common sense.

"Is it possible," he exclaimed, "that this success of yours has n't swelled your head so that you think you 're the greatest actress on earth? Well, you certainly are a remarkable woman. I 've had to do with lots of clever people, but my experience with them is that they show a certain amount of talent, make a little hit and get some notices in the papers, and then the disease of the swelled head attacks them and they never get any further. They seem to take more pleasure in poring over a scrap-book of notices, and telling people how clever they are, than in going straight ahead and making money and fame."

"Well, I've got a swelled head, too," said the girl, quietly, "but it's on what I'm going to do, not what I've done already or what I'm doing now. You don't imagine, do you, Billy, that I'm going to be satisfied with artistic triumphs in Albany and Elmira? No, indeed, dear boy. When we get to New York I'll do something that will make you proud to think that you were the first one to really give me a start; and so you were, for if it had n't been for you I would have been playing *Polly Lightfoot* to this day."

"You forget our friend, Mr. Dillenbeck, when you talk about my giving you your start," rejoined Billy.

"No, I don't," said the girl, quickly. "I wish I could, though."

For a few moments Mr. Freelance regarded her curiously. His experience in the theatrical profession had taught him that clever women of the Maude Wheatleigh type did not always confine their acting to the stage, and he knew, too, how important it was for her to retain his good will and interest at this particular point in her career. At the same time he realized that, taking all things into consideration, it would be better for them both to avoid even the appearance of anything like mutual affection. Luckily or unluckily, Dillenbeck was so wrapped up in himself, so secure in his faith in his own powers of attraction, that he never troubled himself to find out how Maude amused herself during his absence. Mr. Freelance did not often burden his mind with anxiety in regard to Maude's feelings toward him, but now he was conscious of a slight twinge of uneasiness as he asked himself if she were sincere in what she had said about Dolly.

It was Maude herself who broke the silence and diverted the conversation into another channel.

"There's one thing I want to do, though, as soon as I get back to New York," she said, "and that is, make some sort of a start in the way of society. There's no reason in the world why I shouldn't begin to hold my head up a little, now that I've enough money to enable me to dress well and live at a good hotel. I read the society column in the Sunday papers, and there are plenty of actresses whose names appear there constantly. Why, even our old friend, Pearl Livingstone, seems to cut quite a figure in society whenever she's in New York, while in Chicago and San Francisco and places like that she's invited everywhere and meets all the most fashionable people. Don't you think it would be a help to me, professionally, if I were to go out to receptions and parties once in a while?"

Mr. Freelance did not reply at once.

"Well, what do you think of the idea?" she continued, anxiously.

"I don't know why it is," he said at last, "but the social rock is one on which many an artist has gone to pieces. If a woman has been born and brought up in the sort of society that you refer to, and concerning whose doings we read extended accounts in the daily and weekly newspapers, that fact will distinctly prejudice the public against her when she attempts to go on the stage. It will take years of work, backed by great natural ability on her part, to convince the public that she is worthy of even decent consideration. The smart Aleck newspaper men will make it a point to refer to her as an amateur long after she has become a thoroughly accomplished professional; the ponderous satirists of the press will pursue her with elephantine tread; and most of all the public will always be suspicious of her. On the other hand, if a woman has never seen the inside of a decent drawing-room in her life, she will have no difficulty in securing a sort of quasi newspaper indorsement to whatever social pretensions she may set up, no matter how absurd they may be; and I know of no claims of that sort that are more ridiculous than those of Miss Pearl Livingstone, whom I have known intimately for a number of years. I'd like to take you to one of those receptions of hers, just to give you an idea of what society is *not* like, even a little bit. There's nothing to prevent you from going into just as good society as she does, and when we get back to New York I'll introduce you myself, if you like; but I warn you—"

"I'd like it very much indeed," exclaimed Maude, eagerly. "It may not be the best in the town, but it's something, and—and—Billy, I want to know some nice domestic women. Sometimes I feel as if I would give anything to have for a friend some woman of the sort that I used to know when I lived up in the country and did n't know what the inside of a theater was like. I did n't care much for them then, but now I know better; and if I only had for a friend some woman with a nursery full of young ones it would be more to me than anything you can think of."

"Well, if you meet any woman of that sort at one of Pearl Livingstone's soirées you 'll be fortunate," remarked the manager, rising and looking at his watch. "I suppose I 'd better tell Dillenbeck that you won't go to New York." And as he left the room he said to himself, with a sigh, "I suppose I 'll upset my dish again, just as I always do at the critical moment. I 've half a mind to shake the whole concern and get back to New York out of harm's way. It 's better than staying near her to have my heart all torn out by the roots, as it was ten years ago." And then the girl's face, with its look of gratitude, and the moist blue eyes looking into his, came up before him, and he smiled and buttoned his coat tightly across his breast, as if to make sure that his heart did not get away. "Anyway," he said to himself, "if it came to a choice between that wine-opening ape with all his money, and me with nothing but my brains, it's just possible—" And he went off whistling gaily.

He and Maude carried their point, however, and Dolly, unwillingly enough, agreed to postpone the New York engagement until the following season.

## CHAPTER XV

DOLLY remained with the Wheatleigh company until the close of the season, and when he finally returned to New York, after an absence of several weeks, he felt that he had grown immeasurably older and more sagacious by reason of his travels. He was a man of business now, too, holding a five years' contract with Miss Wheatleigh, and having a half-interest in the profits of her tour. This was a matter of no small importance to him, for the rapid pace which he had kept up ever since his advent "on the turf" had made terrible inroads on his fortune, although he could not for the life of him understand how it was that his money went so fast. He said as much to his old friend, Joe Whitcomb, who had now settled permanently in New York; and the latter, who was a shrewd, quick-witted chap, had seen enough during the afternoon they had spent together on Broadway to show him how recklessly the young Crœsus was making his dollars fly.

"It's your extravagance," said Joe, "buying wine for that gang you travel with. I'll bet you not one of them ever puts up a drink when you're in the party; and besides, it must cost you a good deal to play faro and roulette. Just keep account of your expenses for any one day you're in town and multiply it by three hundred and sixty-five, and you'll get an idea of where a good part of your money goes to."

Joe's advice happened to come into Dolly's head as he alighted from a cab at the St. Anthony House on the afternoon of his return to New York, and he determined to follow it, for that day at least.

The news of his arrival spread with marvelous rapidity through the portion of the town which claimed him for its own. General Whiffletree met him with outstretched hands on the very threshold of the café, and the moisture in the old warrior's eyes as he bade him welcome was not a true indication of the condition of his throat. Judge Doonothing, who had suffered from the general drought during Dolly's absence to such a degree that he had twice been on the point of going out to pray for rain, was no less ardent in his greeting; and within half an hour seventeen warm-hearted friends had wrung our hero's hand and accepted his invitation to "sit down and join us."

The old princely feeling came back to Dolly again as he sat in the midst of the joyous company, listening to the words of flattery and endearment that were poured into his ear as freely and generously as he poured the sparkling wine down the parched and husky throats. Again and again were the glasses all charged to do him honor, and again and again did every genial smite the table with his fist and declare with fierce oaths and unusual truth that New York was a brighter and better place than ever now that Mr. Dillenbeck had returned to make glad the hearts of his friends.

It was nearly six o'clock when Dolly rose from the table, surfeited with champagne, but not with flattery, and paid the bar check of $31.50, which item, together with the two-dollar tip to the waiter, he entered in his note-book. His dinner cost him exactly thirty dollars, three of his friends happening upon him by the merest accident just as he was sitting down; and when it was over he returned to the St. Anthony House, where he found General Whiffletree in urgent need of fifty dollars, which he loaned him in a rather weary manner, and escaped through the side-door for fear that Senator Hardscrabble, who was chronically impecunious, would bear down on him with similar intent. It was just half-past ten when he made this last entry in his note-book by the light of a street lamp; and, having but few resources within himself, he called a cab and drove up to a famous gambling-house less than half a mile away, paying one dollar for his ride.

Here he received a welcome that was fully as cordial as that extended to him by his friends in the St. Anthony House, and much more generous, because the proprietor instantly invited him to have a glass of wine—something that his more intimate friends never dreamed of doing. Fortified with his share of a bottle of champagne and a long mild Havana cigar, Dolly ascended to the top floor, gave his hat, cane, and overcoat to an attendant, and then entered the long, well-lighted room where the play was going on. Beside the faro-table sat his friend, Baron Bernstoff, "keeping tab" for the players with an expression of humility on his face that indicated at once to the knowing observer that his last stack of chips had disappeared and he was hoping to profit by the bounty of some more fortunate gamester.

It may be that some of my readers will fail to understand what is meant by the term "keeping tab," and for their benefit I will explain that it is simply a system of marking off on a card, or by means of a box in which are arranged fifty-two buttons, every card dealt from the pack in faro, the object being, of course, to have a check on the dealer. Naturally enough the task cannot be performed in a manner satisfactory to the players by a salaried employee of the gambling-house, so it usually falls to the lot of some impecunious gamester, who, no longer able to take part in the game himself, is forced to content himself with watching the others. Of course none of the great fortunes of this country have been amassed by "keeping tab" in gambling-houses, nor is the occupation one habitually sought by men of recognized wealth and standing in the community; but to a player who has "gone broke" the custody of the box with the thirteen rows of wooden buttons is often a godsend, because it not only gives him an excuse for remaining at the table within sight of the ever-shifting stacks of chips, but also enables him to secure, by close attention to the game, an occasional gratuity in the shape of a stack of whites from some generous winner.

Baron Bernstoff belonged to a class which is much larger in New York than people imagine. A born gamester, he had, after sacrificing to his love of play his inheritance, his position in society and in the army, and his influential friends, been sent to this country by his father, in the vague hope that he might at least bring no further odium on the family name, which was and is one of the most illustrious in Austria. There are scores of men like Baron Bernstoff in New York, and if one wishes to cultivate their acquaintance and put oneself on a familiar footing with a real aristocracy, it can be done with no other passport than a handful of white chips or two or three of the precious blue ones.

The face of the exiled nobleman became radiant with hope as he saw Dolly enter the room, and in his exultation he forgot to mark the cards that were dealt at that moment, until he was sharply reminded of the omission by a player in whom he had been trusting all the evening for a slight gratuity. No sooner had the turn been called and the box emptied of its last card than he left his place at the table and hurried off in quest of his ofttimes benefactor. He found him seated on a high stool in front of the roulette-wheel, with a hundred dollars' worth of chips in front of him.

"Let her go!" cried Dolly, gaily, as he stacked five dollars' worth on the double O.

"Double O in the green," said the dealer, in his monotonous voice, as the ball ceased rolling. Then he swept the board clean, added a stack of blues to Dolly's pile, and started the wheel again.

"Double O, was it? Well, I guess I'll double my stack, then, for luck," cried Dolly, who was in fine feather now.

"Double O in the green, repeater," said the dealer as he swept the board again and handed the fortunate youth three hundred and fifty dollars' worth of chips.

"Well, I seem to be in luck to-night," exclaimed our hero, turning round on his stool and finding Bernstoff behind him. "Baron, how are you? It must have been you that gave me the luck."

"My dear Mr. Dillenbeck," cried the

noble exile as he grasped the other warmly by the hand, "if I cannot bring luck to myself I would rather bring it to you than to any one that I know. Ach, how many times have you been my preserver, and it is *so, so* long since you went away! But luck and I are strangers now, but you— you have luck in everything, women as well as cards. Ah, you sly rascal, I have heard all about you and that beautiful little lady! How beautiful those chips look—what! Really, I am ashamed to take them; but let me once get back to that faro-table and you will have them back before you can win another hundred. Once more you are my preserver, my dear, good Mr. Dillenbeck, and never can I repay your kindness."

This neatly timed flattery had done its work and relieved Dolly of fifty of his easily won dollars. The German returned to his adored faro, and Dolly continued to play with varying fortune until his last chip disappeared into the dealer's maw. It was after midnight then, and he climbed down from his stool, yawned, stretched himself, and told one of the attendants to bring him some brandy and soda.

Of the hundred dollars that he had spent for the elusive celluloid disks there remained to him only the knowledge that Baron Bernstoff had increased his already large indebtedness to the extent of fifty dollars. Taking out his note-book, he found that, including what he had lost and a tip he had just given to the colored attendant, his afternoon and evening had cost him nearly two hundred and thirty-five dollars. Then he remembered Joe's words of advice and multiplied the result by three hundred and sixty-five.

It was the first time since he began to enjoy life that he had paused to seriously count the cost of what he was doing; and now he sat moodily staring at the figures before him, and wondering if it were true that he was wasting his patrimony at the rate of eighty-five thousand a year, in addition to the cost of a very extravagant mode of living. It was true that he owned a half-interest in the forthcoming tour of the Maude Wheatleigh company, but it would be three or four months before he could hope to draw anything from that source, and in the mean time he would be obliged to expend a great deal for new scenery, costumes, lithographs, and other accessories; for he had undertaken to advance all the money necessary for the tour, Messrs. Hustle & Hardup contributing their knowledge of the business, ripe judgment, and cultivated artistic tastes. He had no doubt that his theatrical investment would pay him handsomely in the long run. He only wished that he could go into some other enterprise that would bring him some return — and just at this moment some one touched him on the shoulder, and he heard the Baron's voice: "Come, my dear Mr.

Dillenbeck, let us go downstairs and partake of the excellent supper which is spread for the lucky and the unlucky ones alike. Besides, I have a suggestion to offer you—one that may prove of value to you if you choose to act upon it."

They seated themselves at one end of the long table in the basement, and over a delicious supper, well cooked and properly served, Baron Bernstoff unfolded his scheme, which was sufficiently visionary to enlist Dolly's fancy at once.

"If you were living in Paris, my dear Mr. Dillenbeck," said the Baron, impressively, "you would have a newspaper of your own with which to impress your own individuality on the public. Surely there is no better-known character on Broadway than yourself. Wherever I go I hear of you. Your sayings—are they not on every tongue already? Now why not a paper which shall every week bring articles and poems, and perhaps even pictures, all of which shall be of your *genre?* And besides, just think of the money that you will make after the first two or three months! You will find, my dear Mr. Dillenbeck, that such a journal will have a great *réclame* from the very first."

"Do newspapers of that sort make much money?" inquired Dolly, eagerly.

"Money? They make it by the barrel! I have no doubt that with the subscriptions which would come pouring in, and the advertisements,—which would command a very high price because of your fame as a *viveur* and a man of liberality, —such a paper would pay at least several thousand dollars a month."

Several thousand a month! That was a project that was well worth considering, and Dolly walked home that night with the newspaper idea buzzing in his roomy head.

## CHAPTER XVI

It is probable that the paper-starting microbe, which finds lodgment in the narrowest of brain-cells, had lain dormant in Dolly's soul ever since he came into the possession of his patrimony, and needed only some such invigorating force as the chance suggestion of the impractical German gamester to infuse it with life and cause it to take complete control of the young man's senses.

He talked it over with Miss Wheatleigh and was surprised to see how quickly she came over to his way of thinking, for she was apt to treat his schemes with ridicule and contempt.

He was still more surprised to find that Mr. Freelance, to whom he confided his idea the day after his conversation with the actress, considered the project a fairly good one, and remarked that he had known of people who made fortunes out of weekly journals.

As for his St. Anthony House friends,—Senator Hardscrabble, General Whiffletree, old Rungdown, and the rest,—they asked so many questions and displayed such a kindly and sincere interest in his new enterprise that Dolly was soon convinced that the step which he was about to take was one that would inevitably redound to his credit and make him a still more important factor than he had ever been before in the life of the town.

The fact was that Dolly's friends were, as usual, influenced by purely selfish motives in the interest which they took in his proposed venture. Maude saw in the paper simply another vehicle for the exploiting of her beauty and talents; and besides, she would rather have her backer devote his personal attention to that than to her own affairs, which she knew could be much more satisfactorily handled by Mr. Freelance; while the astute business manager cared very little what his patron did, provided he kept out of the way and did not trouble him with harebrained schemes for the advancement of Miss Wheatleigh's interests — schemes which he was always obliged to accord the courtesy of listening to and apparently considering.

The wine-bibbers rejoiced, as they always did when there was anything new afloat, because starting a paper meant spending more money, some of which ought to fall into their pockets; to say nothing of the various banquets and social occasions which they were sure would mark every stage of Dolly's progress in his new enterprise, as they had in the important work of converting Miss Wheatleigh into a theatrical star.

It should be said of Billy Freelance,

however, that he was at least honest enough to give his chief a few words of timely caution in regard to the conduct of the new publication, and that he even went through the form—and he knew at the time that it was a vain one—of advising him to keep his money in his pocket and not invest it in a business of which he was totally ignorant.

"What did I know about the theatrical business when I started in to back Wheatleigh?" he retorted. "I knew nothing at all, and there were croakers right here on Broadway who said I'd make a failure of it. About the only real friend I had was Whiffletree— Oh, I know you don't like him, so you need n't grin every time his name comes up. Well, he told me to go ahead and not mind what people said, and I'm sure you ought to know whether the girl's a success or no."

For a moment the business manager of Miss Wheatleigh's tour regarded the backer of the enterprise with an expression of pity on his face, and then replied, "Yes, I think the young lady is on the highroad to success; and of course it's entirely owing to you that she's done as well as she has, for of course she's totally destitute of talent and industry, and the people who have managed her have never had any experience and are utterly incompetent, as every one knows. My dear Dillenbeck, the trouble with you is that you have never yet learned to distinguish between the people who try to save money for you and those who do nothing except help you to spend it."

He spoke so seriously that Dolly felt a little bit ashamed of his own self-confident, braggart talk, for he knew well enough that more than once Freelance had saved him from some expensive bit of folly on which his heart was set; and besides, had he not proved a most important factor in the success of the young actress?

"Oh well, you know I appreciate all you've done for her, and for me too," he cried, impetuously, "and that's why I wanted your advice about this paper. Come into the St. Anthony and have a small bottle with me, and we'll talk it all over"—for their conversation had taken place on the Broadway sidewalk, directly in front of that famous place of refreshment.

"A small bottle in the St. Anthony café!" cried Mr. Freelance, with simulated horror. "If I were to be seen drinking champagne there in the bright glare of day everybody would think that the Wheatleigh combination had gone broke. Don't you know that one of the most sacredly guarded traditions of the theatrical business is that no manager must ever be seen drinking wine unless he is on the very edge of bankruptcy? Come around the corner and I'll see if I can take a cocktail with you without affecting the financial standing of the great firm of Hustle & Hardup, with whose interests we are both identified."

Seated at a small table in the back room of a quiet saloon but little patronized by theatrical folk, Mr. Freelance listened attentively while his patron unfolded his scheme for the establishment of a "bright, snappy, live, metropolitan weekly," the very thing, he declared, that New-Yorkers had been waiting for for years—just the thing that they would jump for the very minute it was set before them.

"He's got it bad," said Mr. Freelance to himself as he listened to the other's flow of enthusiasm. He had learned of the plan the night before, and had gone over it with Maude, who said it would be a good thing to have at least one paper in which they could publish anything that they wanted; and as he knew that Dolly's mind was made up, he made no attempt to dissuade him, but satisfied his conscience by urging him to secure some good, hardheaded man as business manager, and some bright young newspaper man as editor.

"Oh, that part of it will be all right," rejoined Dolly, hastily. And as Mr. Freelance went on his way he wondered which of the parasites that hung about his patron would succeed in getting placed on the salary list of the paper.

As for Dolly, he hastened to the St. Anthony café, where he was immediately surrounded by his hangers-on, who seemed to rise up out of the earth the moment he crossed the threshold. All were deeply interested in his new project, and eager to learn from his own lips how soon the first number of the paper was to be issued.

"I'll tell you what it is, my boy," said Senator Hardscrabble as he carefully lowered himself into a big arm-chair, "I've been giving considerable thought to this newspaper project of yours since you first mentioned it to me; and although I was a leetle mite dubious at first, I've just about made up my mind that it's going to be even a bigger success than your theatrical enterprise, and we all know how that charming actress of yours has caught the public fancy. Now if you've only got nerve enough to stand up and face the music you'll come out all right in the end, and I can answer for it that not one of your friends here will desert you so long as they can lift a hand to help you."

The Senator paused and blew his nose on his red bandana handkerchief, while a murmur of approval, emphasized by several ponderous blows on the table, ran through the company.

"I can vouch for every gentleman present, I believe," said Judge Doonothing, pompously, "when I corroborate the assertion of Senator Hardscrabble that your friends—your *true* friends, understand me—will rally about you and give their heartiest support to your enterprise."

Dolly was deeply affected by this display of unselfish loyalty on the part of his friends, and proposed that they should all join him in drinking to the success of the undertaking; and so sincere were his well-wishers in their determination to serve him that not one of them shrank from the ordeal.

"Have you fixed upon a name yet?" inquired Mr. Rungdown.

"A great deal depends upon the name," observed the Judge, in tones suggestive of great native sagacity, quickened by close observation and profound thought.

"I'm going to call it the *High Roller*," said Dolly. "How does that strike you, Judge?"

"Admirable," cried that hoary master of jurisprudence, "and particularly applicable to a paper published by a young man who has shown himself to be one of the finest specimens of the genus high roller that the town has seen within my recollection.— Gentlemen, I call upon you all to drink to the success of the two high rollers, T. Adolphus Dillenbeck, Esq., whom we all know and love, and the new journal by means of which it is his purpose to impress his individuality upon the entire country.— Mr. Dillenbeck, your very humble servant, sir."

The toast was drunk with much enthusiasm, and then Dolly ordered another bottle of champagne, and returned thanks with so much eloquence and feeling that Senator Hardscrabble and Mr. Rungdown sniffed audibly, while the Judge grasped his hand and, squeezing it firmly within his own huge paw, wrung it heartily and murmured, "God bless you, my dear boy; you 'll never want for a friend so long as I am above ground"— which was an unusual display of feeling for that self-contained jurist.

Just at this moment General Whiffletree entered the café and took a hasty and anxious survey of the people assembled therein. His face clouded as his eye fell upon the group at the table, for he did not like to have his dear friends the Judge and the Senator obtain too strong a hold on his particularly dear young friend, Mr. Dillenbeck. He was in a rather ungracious mood, therefore, when he dropped into the only vacant chair at the table; nor did his good humor return when he saw that the bottle was empty and all the glasses were freshly filled—a circumstance due to the hasty precaution of Mr. Rungdown, who had noted his approach. As for Dolly, he was so deeply engrossed in his talk with the Judge and the Senator, who sat one on either side of him, that he scarcely noticed the new arrival, and so it happened that for the space of fully two minutes the old warrior sat silent and fuming, looking enviously at the wine sparkling in the glasses, and wondering suspiciously if his friends were trying to acquire undue influence over the youth who did so much for them all.

Presently the General uttered a sort of dry bark, his usual signal of distress, and one with which even the waiters were familiar; but as that failed to elicit any response he leaned across the board and said in aggressively distinct tones, "Well, Mr. Dillenbeck, you seem to have some very important business on hand this afternoon?"

"We're just talking over that newspaper scheme," replied Dolly, carelessly, for he was intent on what he was saying and did not care to be interrupted.

"What are you going to call her?" demanded the General, brusquely, for he was determined to force himself into the conversation.

"The *High Roller*," replied the other.

The General uttered a snort of suppressed rage, which did not escape the ears of the other guests, although Dolly was so much interested in his own rapid flow of words that he did not hear it. Three things contributed to General Whiffletree's fevered condition of mind: he felt that he had been neglected, if not actually snubbed; he was dry while others near him were partaking of refreshment; and he realized that Dolly, whom he had always regarded as his own special protégé or discovery, had taken an important step without consulting him. Some one—the Judge or the Senator, probably—had suggested the name, for he surely could not have thought of it himself.

"Well, of all fool names that I ever heard of in my life that is the very worst," exclaimed the old man, bringing his fist down on the table with a loud bang as he spoke. "Who ever put it into your head to call it such a thing as that? Why, a paper called the *High Roller* would be laughed out of the town, sir, the first day it was seen on the news-stands."

A sudden hush fell upon the group gathered about the table. Every eye was turned on the blustering and indignant Whiffletree and then upon Dolly, whose face was rapidly changing from an angry red to the ghastly white which indicates a sudden and bitter wrath. If the Prince of Wales had been openly insulted in the Marlborough Club the speechless consternation could not have been greater. The most sacred laws of professional geniality had been brutally violated, and that, too, by one of the most accomplished and distinguished genials that ever fattened at another's cost.

Adolph, the waiter, hovering ever watchfully, as was his wont, within hail of Dolly's eye, heard the General's strident roar, and leaned against a heavy armchair with white face and trembling limbs. That the old soldier had suddenly gone crazy he did not for a moment doubt, and an awful fear came over him that in his delirium he would inflict upon the open-handed young *viveur* some bodily harm which might drive him forever from the café. What if the poor boy were to be killed before his very eyes — and not half his fortune spent, if current rumors were to be credited! Adolph's brain reeled. In all his twenty years' experience as a waiter he had never known any one to question either the honor, the veracity, the motives, or the wisdom of a man who was in the very act of treating his friends to champagne. Disputes had occurred over beer or whisky, but he was sure that the history of the St. Anthony café contained no record of such an assault upon the good taste and sagacity of a gentleman who had already ordered two bottles of wine and was good for as many more before the end of the session.

A professional genial of General Whiffletrec's standing who could be guilty of such a breach of bar-room etiquette was capable of murder, and Adolph breathed a silent prayer that the blow might fall on any head but that of the gilded youth whose tips would in a few months complete the sum needed for the purchase of the little vineyard in the south of France on which the alert and silent servitor had long since set his heart.

Years afterward, while sitting in the shade of the fig-trees belonging to that long-coveted vineyard, the gray-haired ex-waiter described to his friends gathered about him the rush of emotions which overpowered him on that fateful afternoon in the Café Saint Antoine, when *le gros Général* Whiffletree insulted his friend and patron, "*le bon petit Américain à qui je dois même cette propriété.*"

"Why the deuce did n't you consult me before you made such an ass of yourself?" continued the General, querulously; and then, seeing for the first time the pallor on Dolly's face, he paused and began to mop his face nervously with his handkerchief.

Then Dolly Dillenbeck, from his place at the head of the table: "General Whiffletree, I have come here for the purpose of talking over certain matters of business with my friends, and I must beg that you will not interfere in our deliberations. If you have any suggestions to offer I shall be glad to hear them at some future time. —Adolph, another bottle of the same; and, by the way, see here one moment." He whispered a word in the waiter's ear, and then resumed his conversation in an undertone with the Judge and the Senator.

The General made no further remark, for there was a certain note—cold and hard—in the young man's voice that he had never heard before, and he did not know exactly what to make of it. He thought he would say nothing further until after the champagne had been consumed, by which time he thought that Dolly would be in a better frame of mind; and he knew that his throat was in a terrible state for lack of moisture.

"Well, Senator, shall we drink to the success of the *High Roller?*" cried Dillenbeck, gaily, as Adolph deftly removed the cork and filled up the glasses.

"To the *High Roller*, my boy, and may it always be a credit to you," said Senator Hardscrabble, raising his glass with elaborate courtesy.

"Hold on a minute," cried General Whiffletree; "this rascal forgot to bring me a glass."

And now came Adolph's opportunity He had always hated the old man for his bullying ways, and despised him as only a well-trained servitor can despise a man who invariably eats and drinks at the expense of his friends. He had him at his mercy now, and the voice in which he addressed him was perfectly audible to everybody at the table, and perhaps to those at the adjoining tables: "I beg pardon, sir, but Mr. Dillenbeck particularly directed me to serve only those gentlemen who were drinking with him before you came, sir."

The other genials heard, and their hearts were glad. To them the *High Roller* was simply a trough at which they would feed, and now there would be one snout the less to plunge in it.

"Here's to the *High Roller* and the king of all the high rollers," they shouted jubilantly, as they drained their glasses.

"Thank you, gentlemen," said Dillenbeck, significantly. "I'm glad to know who my *real* friends are."

General Whiffletree arose, pushed back his chair, and stalked away without a word.

## CHAPTER XVII

Dolly Dillenbeck plunged into his new enterprise with the eagerness and enthusiasm of a school-boy intent upon the time-honored feat of putting red pepper on the stove. Senator Hardscrabble and Judge Doonothing kindly offered to take a great deal of the work off his hands, and agreed to meet him every evening at half-past six in the St. Anthony café and report progress. The selection of this hour for the daily consultation proved a peculiarly happy one, as it usually resulted in an invitation to dinner, which they never refused, no matter how pressing their engagements might be.

Dr. Puffe was so impressed with the brilliant prospects of the new journal that he lost no time in seeking out its projector and offering his services as editor, although it involved the abandonment of a wide and lucrative connection with various weeklies to which he was in the habit of contributing paragraphs, chiefly of a flattering personal nature. At the advice of his two chief advisers Dolly installed him in the post, and he instantly began to draw his salary. Fine offices were leased in a building conveniently near to upper Broadway, and furnished in an appropriate manner with tasteful and costly furniture. At least eight roll-top desks were included among the articles bought for the staff of the *High Roller*, and two of these were promptly appropriated by Dolly's two elderly advisers. The office soon became the headquarters for the innumerable band of followers that the simple-minded young Crœsus had gathered about him during his brief career; and so many were the callers who wished to give suitable expression to their cordial feelings that Judge Doonothing induced his patron saint to fit up a small office as a sort of miniature café, and stock it with a choice assortment of liquors, cigars, crackers, canned meats, and other light refreshments.

"There!" exclaimed the Judge as he surveyed the rows of bottles and cans, the ice-chest, the cases of claret and champagne, and the huge demijohn of fine old Bourbon whisky; "that's the sort of closet that a gentleman should always keep if he's able to. Now if a gentleman happens to drop in for a social call you can entertain him in a suitable manner, and maybe invite him to take a bite of something, if it happens to be around lunchtime. You'll find that this little closet will go a long way toward making the office popular; and the more people there are who drop in here in the course of the week, the more there'll be to boom the paper and talk it up wherever they go. Why, just among my own circle of friends in the hotels along Broadway I've talked the *High Roller* up till they're all crazy about it. I tell you, when that first number comes out there'll be a perfect stampede after it all through the town."

The words of the veteran jurist were prophetic; for, from the moment of the establishment of the refreshment department, the throng of visitors steadily increased, until the number of well-wishers became so large that Dolly felt sure that the paper would leap at once into unbounded popular favor.

Among the other surprising and encouraging phenomena which helped to keep his spirits up at this time was the discovery of latent literary talent among certain friends of his whom he had never suspected of any such accomplishment. Mr. Rungdown speedily developed a passion for writing reminiscences of that fortunate dramatic era with which his own fame as a Shakespearian actor was indissolubly connected, and solemnly assured Mr. Dillenbeck that the publication of these memoirs would awaken a perfect tidal-wave of interest and enthusiasm among all the "old-timers" on Broadway.

"I'm an old newspaper man myself," said Senator Hardscrabble, cheerily, as he balanced a large sardine on a bit of cracker and then bolted it at a single gulp, "and I'm getting up a few little spicy stories that'll set 'em all wild."

Since the opening of the office buffet the Senator had taken most of his meals there, incidentally making fearful havoc with the demijohn of Bourbon whisky; while in feats with plate and glass the Judge kept even pace with him.

"My boy," said that eminent jurist, in a burst of confidence, "just wait till you read some of the bright, snappy paragraphs I'm getting up for you—meat in every one of 'em. Why, I can remember the time when Major Noah and I used to write the bulk of the matter in his *Sunday Times*, and a fine scholarly sheet it was, too, in those days, I can tell you."

Dr. Puffe went through the form of reading the contributions of the three "old-timers," and pronounced them excellent, thereby obeying one of the cardinal laws of genialdom, which makes it obligatory for a genial to do a favor to another genial in every instance in which the cost falls upon somebody else's shoulders. Of course no true genial will ever trouble himself to help or serve any one at his own expense. There was not one of Dillenbeck's friends who was not the most obliging creature in the world when it came to getting that amiable young man to do something for somebody who could in turn do something for somebody else.

So it came to pass that before the first number of the *High Roller* was ready for the press its projector found himself the possessor of a large quantity of manuscript, for which he had paid handsomely in advance, and which was obviously intended to interest and please the "old-timers," as its authors were pleased to designate their few mildewed contemporaries.

The first number of the *High Roller* was indeed a noteworthy production. Its front page contained a portrait of Maude Wheatleigh,—thanks to Freelance, it was an excellent likeness and a decent piece of artistic work,—and accompanying it was a sketch of the young woman's professional career, written in Dr. Puffe's most fulsome style. Judge Doonothing's "snappy paragraphs" occupied about two columns of space and were marked by a distinctly "old-time" flavor. Many of them bore pleasant testimony to the excellence of the liquors and meats served at various places of refreshment situated within easy reach of the office.

Senator Hardscrabble's contribution, entitled "Personal Reminiscences of a Statesman," betrayed a close familiarity with the legendary lore of Arkansas, and also with American humorous literature of the bar-room and almanac schools. The page devoted to theatrical affairs bristled with portraits of actors and managers, and was made up largely of puffs of those people whose connection with playhouses enables them to have a voice in the distribution of free tickets. The leading article on this page — a leaden-footed essay on "The Stage of Edmund Kean's Time" — bore the signature of Horatio Rungdown; and there was another sketch from his prolific pen, printed in another part of the paper, entitled "Old-time Theatrical Chop-houses, and the Actors who Frequented Them."

There was a literary department in the *High Roller*, and in this number it was filled up with an article called "Men and

Women who Have Made New York the Literary Center of the Continent," and signed by one of the most depraved literary hacks in the town. In this case the writer had simply puffed every one who had anything whatever to do with the purchase of manuscript in magazine or publishers' offices; and so thorough was his mastery of the subject in hand that he had contrived to mention not only the great lights of literature, but also a large number of obscure employees whom he had found to have some very slight influence in the selection of matter.

There was also a department called "Up and Down Broadway," consisting of paragraphs beginning, "Happening to meet Sewer-inspector McElroy in the corridor of the Van Dyke House the other evening," or "Coroner Pigeontoes, the well-known *raconteur*, entertained a choice party of friends in one of the private rooms of the St. Anthony House the other evening, and told the following 'good one' on Charley Ginfizz, who was present, of course." This interesting and instructive page was also rich in anecdotal lore concerning the remarkable things that actors, actresses, and managers did when not engaged in their professional duties. Miss Birdie Marigold, of the "Scuttle of Coal" company, who was "contributing to the leading magazines and reviews"; genial Treasurer Knockdown, who was fond of "rooting" at base-ball games; whole-souled Manager Freepass, who was noted for his courteous attention to the press; comedian Alf Rocks, the famous practical joker—these and a dozen more of the important characters who help to make the world go round on its own axis had their place in "Up and Down Broadway."

There was also a circumstantial account of the last performance in which Edwin Forrest took part, "now printed for the first time," and compiled by the "odd

"The pop of the cork awoke Mr. Rungdown."

genius" who had acted as gasman of the theater on that fateful night.

The paper was well displayed at the news-stands on upper Broadway, and eagerly bought by every one who had designs of any sort on the pocket of its proprietor. When that fortunate and self-confident young man took his afternoon walk on the day of publication he was warmly congratulated by scores of his followers on the handsome appearance of the *High Roller*, the beauty of the picture which adorned its front page, the cleverness shown in its editorial paragraphs, and the spicy flavor which marked its dramatic department. There were even those who professed a deep interest in the published reminiscences of Messrs. Hardscrabble, Doonothing, and Rungdown, each one of whom, by the way, possessed the fatal "old-time" gift of never remembering anything that was of the slightest consequence to anybody.

The only ones who criticized the new journal were Joe Whitcomb and Mr. Freelance, and they were both outspoken in condemning nearly everything that it contained.

"The paper is amateurish—and even worse than amateurish—from cover to cover," said Freelance, contemptuously. "You've let those doddering old fools fill the whole thing up with their recollections of bar-rooms and things that happened before the war. The trouble is, you think that anybody who can make marks on paper with a pen is capable of writing an interesting article. If your tooth ached you wouldn't ask Judge Doonothing to pull it out, would you? If you wanted a new overcoat you would get a tailor to make it. You wouldn't be seen on Broadway with a garment cut and made by old Rungdown, would you? But you let them write all your paper through, and a pretty mess they've made of it. Let me tell you, my young friend, that writing, either for newspapers or magazines, is a profession, and a very difficult one, too. It takes a great deal longer to learn how to write than it does to learn how to cut clothes or pull teeth; and, moreover, there are people in this town who could n't learn to write if they were to work at it for twenty years. Judge Doonothing is one of that class, and Rungdown is another. You take my advice and fire those old stuffs out of your office. Then employ men who make their living by writing to take their place, and at least you 'll have a paper that won't be a disgrace to your name."

"Well, is n't that 'Up and Down Broadway' column all right? I 'm sure it 's all good, timely matter—" began Dolly, but the other interrupted him.

"Timely! Yes, it 's about as timely a collection of puffs as I ever saw in my life. That 's a pleasant reference to 'Socks the popular hatter,' and a very timely one, too, for somebody. Then there's a snappy paragraph about 'Major Rickey, the genial compounder of sours and cocktails, whose cheery face, bright smile, and glorious handshake'—in other words, somebody is getting credit in a bar-room by means of your paper. You ought not to allow any one to be puffed in your paper without your special permission. Make fun of everybody and everything in the town, and the *High Roller* will gain a circulation. Fill it full of these pleasant references to dealers in cocktails, theater tickets, hats, and other light commodities, and you'll drop every dollar you put into it and be laughed at by the very people you've been puffing."

"Is there anything in the paper that pleases you?" inquired Dolly, with mock humility.

"Yes," replied the other as he turned over the leaves; "I don't see anything from the pen of General Whiffletree. How did you come to neglect him? I'm sure he ought to write extremely well by this time—he's had such a fine training for a literary career."

"The fact is," said Dillenbeck, with a little hesitation, "the General and I have n't been as friendly lately as we used to, and he has n't sent in anything yet—"

"Well, don't let him; and if you've quarreled with him accept my congratulations and be careful not to make up with him."

Dolly's heart was touched whenever he thought of his old friend, to whom he had not spoken since the occasion of their falling out in the café, to which due prominence has already been given in these pages. From the moment of the humiliation to which he had been subjected by the young man whom, as he tearfully declared, he had "adopted and treated like a son," the General had scarcely been seen in his old haunts, and how he contrived to live now that he had lost his principal source of revenue was a question that was asked a great many times a day by those who were familiar with his career.

## CHAPTER XVIII

Mr. Freelance had gone to Canada on a fishing-trip, Dolly was spending Sunday out of town, and Maude Wheatleigh was walking slowly up Broadway, wishing that she had some one to talk to. It was a bright, clear morning, just cool enough to make walking on the shady side of the street a pleasant exercise; and our heroine had just made up her mind to go up to Central Park and spend an hour under the trees, when a tall, well-built young man, with a very brown face, stepped directly in front of her and took off his hat.

"Good gracious, Billy, I *am* glad to see you! When did you get back?" cried Maude, wringing his hand with so much vehemence that one or two passers-by turned to look at her, and Mr. Freelance said:

"Walk down the street with me a moment, for I've got an invitation for you for to-night. How would you like to go to an elegant society reception? We're both of us invited, and if you want to go I'll call for you."

"A reception!" cried Maude, delighted at the thought of having some part, no matter how slight, in the social life of the town. From the period of her apprenticeship in Miss Thimbleton's dressmaking-shop in Maplefield she had cherished in her secret heart a dream of social triumphs — a dream which had grown more distinct as she learned more of the world, and which had been fed and pampered by constant reading of the society columns in the daily newspapers. Well as he knew, or thought he knew, the brilliant young actress, Mr. Freelance would have been amazed if he could have known how familiar Maude was with the members of the principal families of the city. She had taken many a long solitary walk for the purpose of gazing at the great houses in which famous balls and dinners were given. She had kept track of all the marriages, divorces, and deaths that had served to heighten or disturb or interrupt the social pageant of the town, so that at this point in her career she was thoroughly well qualified to join in an intimate conversation with the most distinguished leaders of fashion without running the risk of treading on any sacredly guarded toes, or by some maladroit remark letting any dreaded family skeleton loose upon the company.

Her artistic ambition was a high one, but it was feeble in comparison with the intense yearning for a foothold in the splendid world of fashion that had grown within her till she felt that it must be satisfied by some sort of a realization.

Perhaps the opportunity had come to her at last. "Who could have sent me an invitation to a reception?" she inquired, trying to hide her eagerness from the keen perceptions of the manager.

"Guess!"

"How can I guess, Billy? It must be some friend of yours, for *I* don't know anybody likely to give a reception—"

"Oh yes, you do. It's an old friend of yours—Pearl Livingstone by name. I met her on Broadway to-day, and she was as sweet and cordial as it's possible for a woman to be. She fairly took my breath away with her politeness."

"You've certainly taken away mine," rejoined Maude; "but do tell me how she came to ask us, and particularly me, to a reception."

"Well, my own opinion is that she wants to play with Hustle & Hardup again, or it may be that she would like to be on good terms with me for some reason or other—you can bet she wants something or she would n't take the trouble to be civil; but at any rate she stopped me on Broadway and asked about you, and wound up by saying that she had invited two or three friends—her 'society friends,' she said—to her flat to-night, and she hoped I 'd come and bring you with me. Would you like to go?"

"Of course I would," replied Maude, eagerly. "What dress shall I wear?"

Her heart was glad at the prospect of meeting some real "society people" of the sort that her professional associates were always talking about, and of whose comings and goings she was wont to read with so much avidity on Sunday mornings the very first thing after her regular hunt through the dramatic columns for paragraphs about herself. In spite of her manager's sneering remarks about Miss Livingstone's social pretensions she firmly believed that the apartment occupied by that actress during those periods of time which she spent in New York was really the favorite resort of men and women eminent in the social world, as well as those who had won distinction in art—dramatic, plastic, and pictorial—and letters.

"What do you think I had better wear?" she repeated, anxiously. "If I had time I'd have something handsome made expressly for the occasion, for I don't think I've got a single evening dress that's fit to be seen."

"Evening dress!" exclaimed Freelance, awaking from his dreams. "You're not going to a ball at Delmonico's, but to Pearl Livingstone's flat, and any dress you've got will answer. She'll probably receive her friends in that wrapper that we used to be so familiar with. As it's more than likely that I'll be sent out for a pitcher of beer in the course of the elegant festivities, I think I'll wear the clothes I've got on now."

"You'll wear a dress-suit if you go with me," retorted Maude. "And for all you say about Pearl Livingstone, she *does* know some real nice people, and they're liable to be at her flat to-night, so we might just as well be prepared for them. I shall wear the prettiest gown I have, I can tell you that."

"Well, I must be off, for that man on the corner there is waiting to see me about the lithographs," said Mr. Freelance, holding out his hand. "I'll call for you a little before nine."

"Wait a moment, Billy," said the actress, with a slight embarrassment of manner; "there's something I want to tell you—"

"You can tell me to-night," replied the other, hastily. "I can't stop a moment now."

"Very well, then; but remember, when you come up to-night don't send up your card, but come into the ladies' reception-room on the ground floor and you'll find me there."

Freelance walked hurriedly away, and Maude resumed her stroll, apparently engrossed in anxious thought. "I think I'll not tell him until after the reception," she said to herself at last.

# CHAPTER XIX

At nine o'clock that evening Miss Maude Wheatleigh, escorted by Mr. Freelance, was welcomed graciously by Miss Pearl Livingstone at the threshold of the apartment in which, according to all trustworthy accounts, that favorite emotional actress delighted to entertain her many wealthy and distinguished friends. It is a curious and noteworthy fact that although Miss Livingstone is socially unknown in New York, she nevertheless enjoys a high reputation in remote portions of the country as an actress whose profession has proved no bar to her social progress. The whole world, or at least that part of it which lies to the west of the Mississippi, has read of the brilliant gatherings that have made her artistic home the favorite meeting-place of artists, millionaires, statesmen, and poets, who, by the way, are famous for their affinity to one another. That Miss Livingstone had won for herself such an enviable position in the eyes of the polite world was generally attributed to her own exemplary life; but the credit really belonged to Mr. Freelance, who had acted as her press-agent during the early period of her career.

Maude's first feeling on entering the room, of which she had read innumerable descriptions, was one of blank disappointment, which her hostess may have noticed, for she hastened to remark that she was really in no state to receive visitors, as her rooms were all in disorder, and most of her articles of furniture and adornment at the storage warehouse.

Miss Livingstone was attired in a loose gown of light blue, and wore several pieces of jewelry that flashed and sparkled in the gaslight. She had been engaged in conversation with a gentleman of spare build, whose eyes were dark and piercing, and whose clean-shaved face betrayed his calling.

"Let me make you acquainted with Mr. Radcliffe, who is going out with me next season," said Miss Livingstone, after she had greeted her guests; and the actor bowed and said he was pleased to meet them both.

Maude seated herself in a rocking-chair by the window and glanced about her. The furniture seemed to have undergone some hard usage since its purchase in one of the great marts on Fourteenth Street, but it was apparent to her that it must have been at one time tawdry enough to suit the most pronounced theatrical taste. In the rear of the parlor in which they sat was a sort of alcove, partially screened by means of a heavy, striped curtain of the kind termed a "portière" in decorative parlance; and this seemed to be kept in place by four of the dozen brass rings with which it had originally been fastened to the rod of dark polished wood overhead.

Maude looked in vain for the "rare engravings," "choice etchings," and the rest of the artistic paraphernalia that figured in every description that had ever been published of the actress's New York home; but the only pictures that met her gaze were half a dozen photographs of Miss Livingstone herself in various hysterical attitudes, which were conspicuously displayed on the walls and mantelpiece.

The room, however, was not without its artistic significance. Several mad attempts at decoration revealed themselves in the bow of blue ribbon attached to the back of a decrepit chair, and perhaps intended to serve as a danger-signal; in the china plates, embellished with impossible landscapes in pink and blue, and fastened to the walls with brass clamps; in the bunch of forlorn swamp cattails that nodded their dusty heads above the mantelpiece; and in the broken circle of Japanese fans pinned around the base of the chandelier. Half a dozen of these fans had fallen or been pulled down,—Miss Livingstone was holding one in her hand, —and the rest presented a bedraggled and fly-specked appearance that was more likely to awaken the pity of the beholder than to convey an impression of artistic fitness.

There was one ornament, however, which attracted Maude's attention so that she left her seat presently to examine it more closely; and that was a photograph, in a gaudy frame of red plush and gilt, that stood on the upright piano and which she saw Mr. Freelance regarding with a look of amusement on his face. The picture was that of a man of about thirty-five, with features of an unmistakably Hebraic type, crisp, curly hair, parted in the middle with as much precision as if it had been a geometrical problem, a pointed mustache, and a scarf-pin containing what looked like costly jewels.

Maude was still examining the photograph when the door opened and admitted Miss Mabel Morris, in her usual effervescence of good spirits, and a young man who carried a roll of music and a banjo in a cloth bag, and was distinctly "professional" in looks, manner, and speech. Miss Morris greeted both ladies with effusive warmth, and smiled knowingly at Maude as they both recalled the memorable squabble at the card-table on that Sunday morning that seemed, to one of them at least, to belong to the years long gone by.

The young gentleman with the banjo appeared to be on terms of pleasant intimacy with the company, for he addressed his hostess as *Pauline* and Mr. Radcliffe as *Mercutio*, and merrily felicitated Mr. Freelance on the happy tide of circumstances which had enabled him to appear in his own dress-suit and with his own studs in a shirt with collars and cuffs attached, and all on the same evening.

Miss Livingstone giggled audibly at the funny remarks of the newcomer, and then told him to stop his fooling and be introduced to Miss Wheatleigh.

"This is Mr. Slocum," she said, turning to Maude, and then Mabel chimed in: "You may not know it, Charley, but Miss Wheatleigh is an actress, and acts right out on the stage every night and at the Saturday matinée. What's more, she's just made a grand success, and is going out at the head of her own company this fall. She may have a place for you if you show her that you know your business."

Mr. Slocum saluted Miss Wheatleigh with a very low and respectful bow, then gravely removed some of the furniture from the middle of the room and did a "back-fall" of such an irresistibly droll nature that all the guests screamed with laughter, and the actor diffidently remarked that his turn usually went better at matinées and at holidays than in the evening, whereat Miss Livingstone broke out into renewed laughter and declared that Charley was the most ridiculous man she had ever known in her life, and she did wish he would learn to behave when there were ladies around.

Philosophers who have been enabled, by virtue of frequent opportunity and their own gifts of discernment, to study the feminine character with a degree of thoroughness that commands my envy and respect declare that a woman who does not wear her heart on her sleeve, who has perhaps reached maturity with her affections unscarred by the darts of Cupid, is apt to love, if she loves at all, with far more intensity than a woman of normal traits and the usual capacity for affection. According to these thinkers she is also likely to select a much less worthy object for her regard.

This may or may not be true—personally I have very little faith in the studies made of women by men; but it is undoubtedly a fact that a woman whose capacity for the enjoyment of humor is limited, and whose face is habitually cast in a serious mold, will usually fall a victim—I mean in the laughing sense—to some funny man whose humorous methods are of the primitive and broadly acrobatic type which I have tried to indicate in describing Mr. Slocum. Miss Livingstone was distinctly lacking in the humorous sense, as nearly all egoists and egotists are. It would have been impossible for her to have discovered anything funny in the published writings of Sterne or Oliver Wendell Holmes; but when Mr. Slocum turned a handspring or repeated the hackneyed facetiæ of his calling she found it simply impossible to control her merriment.

On the other hand, Miss Wheatleigh possessed a really keen sense of humor—a quality, by the way, which is not nearly so rare in her sex as certain philosophical students of womankind would have us believe. Women are not usually creators of humor, but their appreciation must be very keen, for they not only laugh immoderately at genuine wit, but also derive great enjoyment from plays and books in which I, for example, can find no sort of fun. Miss Wheatleigh's sense of humor had been greatly developed by her intimate association with Mr. Freelance, and although the actor's buffoonery did not seem to her particularly comical, she could not help laughing heartily at the spectacle of the usually dull and serious-minded Livingstone bursting with uncontrolled and hysterical mirth. Mr. Freelance seemed to think it funny too, and they both roared so heartily that Mr. Slocum knew that he had made a great hit, and determined to name seventy-five dollars a week as the price of his professional services.

Maude seated herself beside her hostess, and the two were soon in the midst of a conversation that was to all appearances affectionate and intimate.

"I expected some of my society friends this evening," said Miss Livingstone, in low, confidential tones, "but just before you came in I got a note from Mrs. Judge Cauliflower saying that she was unavoidably detained. It's really too bad, for I would be pleased to have you meet her. You've heard of Mrs. Cauliflower, of course?"

"No, I don't think I have," replied Maude, wondering how such a name could have escaped her in her diligent studies of New York society as reflected in the Sunday newspapers.

"No?" resumed Miss Livingstone, with

a note in her voice that meant: "To be sure you have n't. How stupid of me to forget that you never had the opportunity to meet people like the Cauliflowers!" Then she continued aloud: "Well, Lydia is a dear good girl, and if she was n't so continually wrapped up in society I would see more of her than I do. But, really, I have very little taste for balls and dinner-parties and all that goes to make up the life of a society woman nowadays. This is where I find rest and enjoyment, Miss Wheatleigh, when I am not working— I should say practising my profession. At one time I went out a great deal, and used to meet hundreds of people whose names I could scarcely recall when I saw them. Now I have a few warm friends, many of whom are sought after constantly by the proudest in the land. Every door, even the most exclusive, is thrown open to them, and yet they seem to find something in this little home of mine that is lacking in the grander palaces that they visit. You ought to have seen the costume Mrs. Cauliflower wore at the Palestine Commandery ball last winter; every reporter gave a full description of it. But, after all, I care more for literature and art than for the gay whirl of society. I do all my writing at that desk by the window, and sometimes I am glad to be alone, so that I can bury myself in my books. With a favorite author in my lap I can—"

"There's a terrible drought here this evening, Pauline," interrupted Mr. Slocum at this moment. "Here's Mabel with her tongue hanging out, and I'm afraid Freelance is suffering pain."

"Somehow you always bring a fearful dusty throat with you when you go out for an evening," said the hostess, seemingly annoyed at this premature call for refreshments. "Well, just open the ice-chest in the next room and get out the beer; or perhaps you want whisky? You'd better ask these ladies what they'll have, too, while you're about it."

Mr. Slocum made his way to the spot in the back part of the flat where the refreshments were cached with a speed born of much practice and long familiarity, and returned bearing half a dozen bottles, from which he dispensed good cheer with considerable native humor. At the same time he disseminated agreeable rumors in regard to a collation which he said the servant was preparing in the kitchen.

"You were just saying something about books," remarked Maude, demurely, as soon as the tumult incident to the serving of the refreshments had subsided. Freelance heard her remark—she had intended that he should—and pricked up his ears. "I remember that you used to be a great reader, and I have often seen newspaper articles about your library. Is it here?"

"Oh dear, no," rejoined the actress, hastily. "I would n't dare keep my books and pictures here; and, besides, I 'm not half settled yet. They 're all at the safe-deposit storage warehouse; that is, all but a few of my favorites." As she said this she turned to a table beside her and took from it the scrap-book which was her constant companion in all her travels, and the celebrated "Garland of Gems," to which allusion has already been made in these pages.

Mr. Freelance smiled broadly as his eyes fell upon the familiar volume, and Miss Livingstone, all unconscious of the fact that she was furnishing entertainment to at least two of her guests, continued: "It was Mrs. Judge Cauliflower who gave me this work. You know she has great literary taste and reads all the principal authors. I went to dinner at her house one night, and you ought to see the style she puts on. Why, she keeps two butlers the year round, and you never see her at any time of the day without diamonds in her ears—"

Miss Livingstone was evidently on the point of making further revelations indicative of the refinement and good breeding of Judge Cauliflower's attractive spouse, but just at this moment there was a knock at the door, and the hostess rose to welcome her friend, Mr. Pointdexter, who was, as she subsequently whispered to Miss Wheatleigh, "one of the principal members of the four hundred."

Mr. Pointdexter, who was a young man of excessively clean and rosy appearance, entered the room with considerable diffidence, and did not seem to be quite sure whether he should take immediate flight or remain permanently. He was attired in evening dress, and had provided himself with so many accessories and embellishments in the way of gloves, studs, rings, key-chain, watch-chain, cape-coat, silk hat, and patent-leather shoes that Mr. Radcliffe and Mr. Slocum looked upon him with a respect that was tempered by keen envy.

"If I had such a dude make-up as that I could act," said Mr. Radcliffe to himself, with some bitterness; for he was billed to play *Gerald Vasavour* in "Fifth Avenue's Darling," and the question of an appropriate wardrobe was looming up ominously on the horizon of his thoughts.

It was probably the first time that Mr. Pointdexter had ever found himself in the company of so many members of the theatrical calling, and this close contact with genius had the effect of increasing his natural diffidence and nervousness. Mabel Morris watched him as he sat gazing with round-eyed wonder upon the guests, and uttered a silent prayer.

"How soon are you going to favor us again with one of your fine performances, Miss Livingstone?" inquired the new arrival, in a low voice.

"I expect to be at the Jollity Theater October 29th in a new piece, and I hope you will be on hand the first night and come back and tell me what you think of it," replied Miss Livingstone, with one of her most amiable smiles.

"A new play! Why, I am sure you will never get anything better than 'Only a Perfect Lady.' Do you know, we were talking about you up at the club last night, and we all thought you were perfectly charming in that."

"Perhaps Mr. Pointdexter will join us in a social drink," remarked Mr. Slocum, who wanted one himself, rising suddenly to his feet and taking a glass and bottle from the table. The newcomer consented, after considerable protest, to partake of a small and weak solution of whisky and water. The others poured out their libations with unsparing hand, and then there was a call for music.

Mr. Slocum responded at once to the

call, playing his own accompaniment on his banjo, and singing two new comic songs of unmistakable British music-hall origin. He was glad enough to have a chance to display his accomplishments in the presence of Mr. Freelance and Miss Wheatleigh, both of whom he recognized as persons of coming importance in the theatrical world.

"Go over to the piano and sing us something, Billy," commanded the hostess. "You'll find plenty of music there that you know, and it is a good while since I heard you troll."

Mr. Freelance did as he was told, and Maude went over to help him find some songs. His eye fell upon the photograph in the plush frame, and he called Maude's attention to it and said in a low whisper, "That's an *objet d'art* that you will find in every soubrette flat in this town."

"Who is he, and what does he do?" asked the other, innocently.

"I don't know what this one's name is, but I rather fancy that his function in life is to pay the rent of this flat," he answered carelessly; "and what's more, if you go back to the time of Hogarth you'll find that there were chaps of this sort around then. They belonged to the same race, too."

"Hello, who's his nibs?" demanded Mr. Slocum, crossing the room as he spoke, and taking the portrait from Billy's hands. "Is that the original Chakey Einstein, Pauline?" he inquired.

"No, sir," responded the hostess, frigidly. "That is a gentleman who could buy and sell you two or three times over without missing it. I'll thank you to put that photograph back where you got it, Mr. Slocum, and not favor us with any more remarks about people whom you don't know and probably never will."

"That gentleman has known me ever since I was knee-high," she explained to Mr. Pointdexter, who was seated beside her. "Maw thinks the world and all of him. He's not in the profession, but in a big business down on Broadway. He's a great society man, and a famous club man, too. He belongs to the Phenix Social Club and all those gilt-edged clubs, and when his regiment gives a ball they always put him on the floor committee. You ought to have seen him at the one they gave last year. He looked perfectly grand. I can remember the time when he used to dandle me on his knee."

"When was that? Night before last?" inquired Mr. Slocum.

"I'll thank you to remember that you're in the company of ladies, Mr. Charley Slocum," cried the actress, angrily. "You need n't put your hands up behind your ears like that! My friend may be a Hebrew, but if he is he's a dead white one, and his religion does n't concern either you or me. He's a great spender, too, and that's more than you are."

Miss Livingstone was rapidly becoming angry, Mr. Pointdexter was looking very uncomfortable, and Mr. Slocum seemed to be meditating still more exuberant flights of humor, which might have borne unpleasant results had not Mabel Morris interfered so peremptorily that the comedian sat down in a corner, while Pearl, with flushed cheeks, proceeded to entertain Mr. Pointdexter with a flood of anecdote relating to the many noble traits and generous exploits of the gentleman whose photograph stood in its attractive plush frame on the piano.

Very soon Mr. Freelance discovered among the tattered and well-pawed relics of Miss Livingstone's musical career some songs that he knew. He sang one of them, and sang it very well, too, as even Mabel Morris, who played his accompaniments and had a remarkably quick and keen musical ear, admitted. His voice was a high, clear baritone, of the kind that is usually described as a "tenor robusto" when its possessor happens to sing in grand opera, and is known as a "pure tenor, of great strength and sweetness," when it belongs to the principal member of a comic-opera company. It was not often that Mr. Freelance consented to sing, and to-night Maude was surprised at a certain sympathetic, touching quality in his voice which she had never noticed before, and which brought tears to her eyes as she listened. She wiped her eyes hastily, and was conscious the next moment that the singer had observed her action.

Mr. Freelance's music was received with so much genuine enthusiasm that he probably would have been asked to sing again had not the appearance of the servant with a large tray of refreshments turned the thoughts of the guests into another channel. There was a very nice lobster salad prepared by the hostess herself, crackers and cheese, beer, whisky, ginger-ale, syphons of carbonated waters, and cigarettes; and all went even merrier than the average marriage-bell until they had reached a late stage of the repast. Then the hostess, who had been patiently biding her time, turned to Mr. Freelance, who sat at her left hand, and said: "And so Miss Wheatleigh is really married to young Mr. Dillenbeck after all? I have n't had the heart to speak to the poor girl about it, because—well, we all know she has acted rather foolishly, and now he's run through all his money and can't do anything more for her. I heard the other day" (here she ostentatiously lowered her voice) "that he was beginning to act a little foolish. Well, really, I hope it's not true, for her sake. But, Billy, I always thought you were mashed on her yourself; you ought not to have let that fellow get ahead of you!"

In spite of all his efforts to sit perfectly quiet and maintain an air of calm indifference, Billy Freelance winced under the words of the emotional actress—winced visibly, too, thereby making glad her heart; for she had waited all the evening her chance to tell him what she had learned on mere hearsay a week before. Indeed, it is not unlikely, such was the craft and malevolence of the woman, that she had invited them both to her rooms that night for the express purpose of telling him about Maude and then gloating over his misery.

The venom of the serpent's tooth lurked beneath Miss Livingstone's apparently simple and friendly words. Freelance had often imagined that his star would eventually marry the man to whose liberality she was indebted for the great opportunity of her life, and this belief was materially strengthened by his knowledge of the fact that Dolly had still another fortune—that of his mother—to spend. But he had never for a moment suspected that the marriage had actually taken place, and a fierce feeling of resentment came over him at the thought that she should have taken such a step without consulting him.

"And so that was why she seemed to hesitate this morning when I spoke of coming here, and that was what she was going to tell me? Well, I'll not give her the chance to tell me; I'll let her know that I heard it myself first."

Then there was that careless reference to Dillenbeck's condition. That the career of extravagance and debauchery followed by that foolish young man had seriously undermined his health, as well as his fortune, Mr. Freelance had known for some time; but that the meteoric wine-opener was growing weak-minded and foolish to a degree that was likely to attract attention before long was a piece of intelligence that had not yet reached his ears, although he himself sometimes feared that the decay of his mind had actually begun.

As he and Maude were walking home the actress remarked: "That was funny about that photograph. I thought I should die laughing when she tried to tell us what an elegant gentleman her friend was. Is there really some Hebrew of that sort enshrined in every soubrette flat in the city?"

"No," rejoined Mr. Freelance, with a significant look; "I've heard of one or two flats in which a Christian gentleman has the precious privilege of paying the rent."

The contempt expressed in the young man's voice and in the look that he cast down at his companion made her almost writhe with chagrin and a sense of degradation. She should have told him of the marriage herself, and not permitted him to learn it from the lips of that spiteful woman. What would become of her now if he were to leave her? The mimetic power which, in her peculiar organization, had been developed largely at the expense of heart and conscience came to her rescue, and, clasping his arm with both her hands, she exclaimed, in a voice choking with emotion,— the same voice which earned her a recall at the close of the second act, a voice which she hoped would some day win for her still greater renown than she had ever known before,— " Billy, for God's sake, don't talk to me like that! Dolly and I have been married for three weeks, but it must be kept a secret. I could n't help it. Believe me, Billy, I could not."

# CHAPTER XX

EVERYTHING in this world has its uses, and the "secret marriage" is no exception to the rule. I have long regarded it as a most admirable institution—not in real life, by any means, but as a convenient device for the writers of romances. What the Humphry Davy safety-lamp is to the miner, the clothes-wringer to the housekeeper, the "secret marriage" is to the novelist or story-teller. It can be made to cover a multitude of sins. Interposed between a risky situation and the prejudices of the average American reader, it is frequently the very salvation of a story. It is the life-boat of fiction; but in real life it is generally deplorable and inexcusable.

These remarks, however, do not apply to the secret marriage which I have recorded in the preceding chapter. That has been introduced into these pages, not as an expedient or as a sop to the moralists, not as a protection from the slings and arrows of outrageous Philistinism, but simply and solely because it was an actual occurrence in the lives of those whose career I am setting forth.

Maude and Dolly were united in a legal and binding marriage for reasons which are simply inexplicable to me, the chronicler of their various mishaps and achievements. I do not know why they chose to keep the matter a secret, any more than I know why they were married at all. I only know that the ceremony was performed by a duly licensed preacher, and the affair managed with so much secrecy that it was fully two weeks before news of it reached the ears of Miss Pearl Livingstone; and I have already told how malevolently that distinguished actress made use of her knowledge. She had more than one reason for wishing to break up the intimacy between Maude and Freelance, not the least of which was her desire to enlist the services of the latter in behalf of herself. And then she had found it much easier to forgive him for the part he had taken in the conspiracy to oust her from the Hustle & Hardup Company than to forgive Maude her artistic success and growing popularity.

I have another explanation to make in this chapter of apologies, and it concerns the style of conversation in which many of the characters in this story express themselves. My readers may have noticed that the language employed is not always what one would term Addisonian English, and I am afraid that the impression has gained ground that it is slang.

This is a mistake. It is not slang, but

dialect, that I have put into the mouths of Mr. Freelance, Miss Livingstone, and the rest. It is dialect, and I earnestly hope that my critics and readers will accord to it the respect that belongs to dialect, and not the contumely that is the lot of mere slang.

In the present fertile age of American letters it has been the custom to apply the term "dialect" to any language that intentionally departs from pure Anglo-Saxon, provided it be accredited to some region that lies outside the limits of New York City, or, to be more exact, outside the limits of what is regarded as civilized New York; for there is dialect spoken below Eighth Street and east of Broadway. In the Tenderloin precinct, however, nothing is used but slang.

As for dialect, it may be recorded by Mr. Cable as indigenous to Louisiana, or by Miss Wilkins as indigenous to Connecticut, or by Mr. Ralph as indigenous to the most densely populated quarter of the town; in either case it is dialect pure and simple, and as such entitled, by virtue of the approval of critics, magazine editors, celebrated short-story writers, and other important personages, to rank directly after the queen's English, even as the Archbishop of Canterbury takes precedence of everybody but royalty. But as for poor, common, vulgar slang, as it occurs in nearly all the human strata that constitute upper Broadway, it is a mere city knight, an ennobled tradesman, in the great aristocracy of speech.

I can offer but one excuse for putting so much of this dialect of the town into the mouths of my characters, and that is that it is in precisely such words and phrases as are recorded here that men and women of the sort that I have described are in the habit of making known their wants and expressing such opinions as may find lodgment in their brains.

There are perhaps some who will say, on reading this, that if I make any apology at all it should be for introducing the characters themselves to my readers, who, I am sure, are used to much better company. Well, so am I used to much better company than that which my young hero affects; but it is his story that I am telling, not my own, and those who wish to hear it must necessarily follow its central figure into the sort of society that a young man of inordinate wealth and vanity, great good nature, and limited intelligence would be apt to frequent in a city which has not yet been able to make room for a decent idle class.

I do not need to be reminded of the fact that there are in New York thousands of honorable, high-minded, and intelligent men and women. Indeed, I would gladly introduce a few of them to my reader if for no other purpose than to show that the flash life of the saloon, the theater, and the gambling-house is not the best that the metropolis has to offer. Dolly himself might have known some of these men and women, and perhaps have married some nice young girl belonging to them, and settled down to a life of colorless ease. But he preferred the garish lights of Broadway, the meretricious glitter of the stage, and the flattery of sycophants to anything else in the town, thus making this story possible.

The young man whose career Hogarth has drawn in immortal lines had tastes that were not at all unlike Dolly's, although they found expression in a coarser way, as became a coarser age; and altogether it was a precious company to which the great English satirist introduced those who have watched "The Rake's Progress" through London Town.

It was this similarity between the two careers, separated by a century and a half of time, that greatly impressed Miss

Wheatleigh when she went to the Astor Library, a few days after the reception at Pearl Livingstone's, and sat down with Hogarth's engravings before her to find out what Freelance had meant when he spoke of the photograph in the red plush frame. She made a practice now of quietly looking up every book or picture that he chanced to mention in conversation, and in this way she had managed to scrape a slight acquaintance with certain phases of literature and art, and to acquire, in haphazard fashion, some knowledge of the sort that country folk usually call "book-larnin'," in a tone that indicates some uncertainty in their minds in regard to its real value.

Maude soon came across the picture to which Freelance had referred. It was the one in which the Jew's mistress picks a quarrel with her protector, while the lover, aided by her maid, escapes from the room unobserved. The genius of the great artist appealed strongly to the practical side of her character as well as to the sense of humor which, as I have already noted, had been highly developed by her acquaintance with the cynical Mr. Freelance. She smiled broadly as she examined the picture carefully and thought of Pearl Livingstone and the friend who kindly paid her rent. Then she glanced at the other pictures until she came to "The Rake's Progress," and that set her thinking. It seemed to her that the career set down there, in the minute detail that only Hogarth was capable of, was that of her husband, whom she had left but an hour before, sleeping the heavy sleep of semi-inebriety. The clothes and other accessories belonged to a century long gone by, but the spendthrift himself was Dolly, and the men and women who flattered and pandered to him were so many Whiffletrees and Doonothings, and—"I hope I'm not in that crowd of frowzy-looking women," she said to herself, angrily, as she closed the book with a bang. The thought was not a pleasant one, and as she left the library and walked rapidly uptown she tried vainly to drive it from her mind. There was another picture, almost as unpleasant as this one, which remained obstinately in her memory, and that was the one which depicted the closing scene in the life of the young English rake.

"I don't think Dolly will ever go crazy on his small stock of brains," she said to herself, with more contempt than pity in her heart. And then the hideous reality of the madhouse, and the gay young pleasure-seeker with his head shaved and the leer of imbecility on his face, came upon her with a pointed significance that made her sick at heart. Since her marriage she had been unable to shut her eyes to the fact that Dolly was not exactly what he had been in the days when she first knew him. He acted strangely at times, and had fallen into a habit of talking to himself. He seemed to be short of money, too, which was incomprehensible to her, for from her earliest childhood she had been accustomed to think of the Dillenbeck fortune as inexhaustible. How could this foolish boy have spent it all in such a short time? It troubled her more than the loss of his mind.

She thought at once of Freelance,—as she always did in emergency,—and she wondered whether or no he would withdraw his friendship from her because of her marriage. She would lose no time, but send for him at once, tell him all that she feared, and implore him not to desert her. It lacked but a few weeks of her New York début, and without his strong common sense, managerial skill, and well-tried fidelity to lean on, she felt that it would be useless for her to make her appeal to the heartless, careless, blasé metropolitan public.

Again the picture of the madhouse came back to her. "Women should never look at such drawings as that," she said to herself. "There is too much truth in them to please us. We would rather see the world portrayed as we would like to have it than as it is. I don't think that Hogarth was ever popular with women."

And just then she found herself face to face with Mr. Freelance; for her rapid steps had brought her up Broadway well beyond the St. Anthony House, and the manager was on his way to the office of Hustle & Hardup. He greeted her with calm politeness, and made no reference to what she had told him on the occasion of their last meeting.

"Billy," she said, looking wistfully into his face, "I want to speak to you about Mr. Dillenbeck. Sometimes he does very queer things, and I often wonder how it will all end. His memory seems to be faulty, and this morning I went and looked at those pictures of Hogarth's that you told me about. There was one that was terrible—the last one in 'The Rake's Progress'—the one where he is in the madhouse. I can't get it out of my mind."

She was not acting this time, a fact that Mr. Freelance, who was thoroughly familiar with all her moods and methods, recognized as soon as she began to speak. He shrugged his shoulders in reply, and said, after a moment's thought: "Well, what can you expect? Here's a young man who has been brought up on milk, and jumps from that to champagne and brandy. He's not overstrong, either in body or mind, and he simply can't stand the pace. You're his wife, and if you can't make him pull up and take care of himself the chances are that he won't last much longer. Can't you send him away somewhere for a few months? There are institutions that make a specialty of treating such cases as his."

"I believe that's a very good idea, Billy," said Maude, thoughtfully; "but I'm afraid it will be a very hard thing to persuade him to go. He might do it if we gave him a good scare. Let's take him down to the Astor Library and show him those Hogarth pictures. I know they frightened me."

Mr. Freelance raised his hat and was about to resume his walk, but the actress detained him.

"There's another thing I wish to speak to you about that has worried me for some time," she said, in hesitating tones. "I thought of telling you about it a good while ago, but I felt that you had so much on your shoulders in the way of responsibility and anxiety that it would be wrong to give you anything else to worry about unless it were absolutely necessary."

"What is it?" demanded Mr. Freelance, abruptly.

"Well, the fact is that for some unaccountable reason Mr. Dillenbeck has become very short of money lately, and several times he has come to me for small loans, 'just to carry him through the day,' as he puts it. I don't imagine that he is seriously embarrassed, but I do hope that he will be able to get hold of some ready cash before long, for I can't afford to dip into my savings every day or two, just to keep him in spending-money."

"Dillenbeck hard up?" exclaimed Freelance. "Well, if he's hard up, I'd like to know why he does n't get off the earth. All that fellow was brought into the world for was to spend money; and if he goes 'broke' he 'll find out very soon that the world has no further use for him. But it can't be that he has run through his property already. I remember his father, old Jacob Dillenbeck, twenty years ago, and a close-fisted, hard-headed old miser he was. He was known to be rich, for he had been hoarding all his life; and as he never speculated in Wall Street, or opened wine, or played faro-bank, or tried to pick winners, he must have left a pretty stiff heap when he died. Foolish as that boy has been, I don't see how he could have run through his property during the short time he's been on the town."

"No, I don't think he has," rejoined Miss Wheatleigh. "But you see he's been under a very heavy expense of late, for in addition to his extravagant habits he has had to pay out a great deal of money to keep that silly paper going—and really it must cost him a great deal to run it and pay for all those contributions."

"I thought when he had that row with old Whiffletree that he would have a chance to recoup himself financially, for he was the very worst 'beat' in the whole St. Anthony gang; but I suppose that what he had been spending on the old man he now drops on the *High Roller*, so it amounts to about the same thing."

"He has told me all along that he had a large interest in his mother's estate," continued Maude, "and that as soon as he could realize on it, which would be very speedily, he would have about a hundred thousand in cash. In the mean time, however, we have to live more economically than we used to, and I actually tremble when I think of the money that he will have to spend before the season opens in the fall."

The information imparted to him by Maude made the young business manager very anxious about the enterprise in which he had embarked, and of which Dolly was the financial corner-stone. He went to Hustle & Hardup at once;

but those managers, although generally shrewd and suspicious, were now so elated by their association with the popular young Broadway wine-opener that they laughed at his fears and assured him that young Dillenbeck still had millions back of him. Theatrical managers never talk of anything less than millions, even when no bills of larger denomination than two dollars are passing through their hands.

From the managers' offices Mr. Freelance went directly to the *High Roller* office and bluntly requested Dolly to inform him plainly in regard to his financial condition. He received from the young man the same assurance that he had already given Maude regarding the money that was to come to him from his mother's estate; and, so straightforward and sincere were his words, so apparent was it that he himself firmly believed what he was saying, that Mr. Freelance

"A REMARKABLY NICE LOOKING YOUNG WOMAN."

departed very much relieved in his mind. He was convinced that Dolly had spoken the truth, and although he expected that they would all be cramped for a month or two, he had no doubt that his affairs would eventually be straightened out.

A few days later a whispered rumor reached the alert ears of Mr. Freelance to the effect that young Dolly Dillenbeck had nearly reached the bottom of the heap of gold that but yesterday had been regarded as inexhaustible. This rumor the young manager proceeded to laugh to scorn in such a confident and convincing manner that, for a few days at least, its voice was stilled. Nevertheless the hard times had set in for those who were dependent in any way upon the young Crœsus. The merry band of genials no longer gathered at the St. Anthony House to pound upon the table, chant his praises, and drink his health in the wine for which he paid the reckoning. Poor

Adolph, gloomily calculating that one more month of Dolly would have enabled him to purchase the vineyard on which he had long ago set his heart, now devoted so much of his time to watching the swinging doors of the café, in hopes that the young champagne prince would return again to his kingdom, that the proprietor of the house sharply chided him for his neglect of duty. Whereupon the faithful and industrious servitor burst into a flood of tears and told his employer that unless young Mr. Dillenbeck's custom could be brought back to the café he did not care whether he were discharged himself or not. Once in a while one of Dolly's stray followers would pass through the swinging doors, cast an anxious and thirsty eye about the room, and then vanish; but no one ever thought of waiting twenty-four hours for Dolly to appear, as they had done in the glad days before.

The hard times were felt at the *High Roller* office as well as in the café. The printers' bill was growing steadily from week to week, and the voice of the paper-dealer was making itself heard in accents of pleading, followed by complaint. Even the contributors were beginning to grumble, and Senator Hardscrabble made one or two very pointed remarks about the impropriety of keeping gentlemen waiting for their money. It must be admitted, however, that he spoke under the spur of great affliction, for the barrel that had contained choice Bourbon whisky was empty, and there was no more to be had except for cash.

The office was no longer a pleasant lounging-place for any one, and Dolly contrived to keep away from it as much as possible, leaving the management of its affairs in the hands of Dr. Puffe, who did not care what went into the paper so long as he could collect his salary; and now that that was in arrears his indifference was more marked than ever before.

About this time a terrible discovery was made in regard to the circulation of the *High Roller.* Of the earlier numbers twenty thousand copies a week had been taken by the American News Company and distributed throughout the country (about half of these came back each week), and when the paper entered upon the third month of its existence a check amounting to several hundred dollars was paid by the News Company. Dolly looked upon this check as an evidence of the *High Roller's* prosperity; and so confident was he in his enterprise, so unwilling to listen to the words of any one who did not flatter him, that he did not realize that the public, having satisfied its curiosity in regard to the new publication, had ceased to buy it except by accident, and that the circulation had almost entirely fallen off. Then the American

News Company began to send the returns back by the cart-load, and at the end of the third month poor Dolly found to his dismay that not only was there no money due him from the company, but that he was actually in debt for unsold copies of the earlier editions that had been returned to him.

Maude came home one night and found her husband by secret marriage sitting up in a gaudy, flowered dressing-gown before a table that was strewn with paper.

"I don't know how it is," he said mournfully, as she greeted him, "but this infernal News Company always sends back more papers than it takes. We sent them ten thousand copies this week, and the returns are twelve thousand. I wonder if they've got a printing-press and print them themselves every week?"

"That's one of the principal expenses in a newspaper office," remarked Mr. Freelance, gravely—he had just brought

Maude in from an evening rehearsal—"you're compelled to buy so many papers from the American News Company every week, whether you want them or not. Now I dare say that you could get along very nicely with only one or two hundred copies of this week's issue, but that concern will insist upon making you take twelve thousand, whether you want them or not. I have had my experience with them, and it was always the same story. Sometimes when I wanted money to buy food with I had to spend it on the American News Company, buying papers that I did n't want. Now, if you were to do what I 've often told you to,—that is, put something in your *High Roller* that the people will read,—the company will buy papers of you instead of selling them to you."

"Yes, Dolly," chimed in Maude, "do, for heaven's sake, pay attention to what Mr. Freelance says, and get some one who knows how to write to contribute to your paper. If I were you I would throw that old Hardscrabble and Doonothing and all the rest of them out of doors. What they write positively makes me sick. It's all about bar-rooms and bummers and courteous doorkeepers; and in that column of paragraphs there are always at least three puffs of McSnorley's Square Deal Restaurant. I suppose those old beats are running up accounts there. And, Dolly, do, for heaven's sake, give orders not to mention my name more than once a week. I am afraid to pick up the *High Roller* for fear I'll see some idiotic story about myself, or some ridiculous puff of my talents, badly written, untrue, and calculated to do me more harm than good."

## CHAPTER XXI

"I AM afraid," said Mr. Freelance to Maude one day, as she was deploring her husband's continued excesses, "that we are entering upon a long period of discomfort and financial depression that may end in actual disaster. As you know, the great firm of Hustle & Hardup is chronically impecunious and has not the slightest credit anywhere in the country. The money which must be expended for costumes, scenery, lithographs, advertising, etc., before we begin our season, runs up into the thousands, and where it is to come from I don't know. How soon will that precious husband of yours come into possession of his mother's estate ?"

"Not until he is twenty-seven years old," replied Maude. "I rather imagine that the old lady had a pretty correct idea of his taste for extravagance, and fixed it so that he would have something to fall back on when the rest of his pile was gone."

"Well, the only thing that I can suggest," said Mr. Freelance, thoughtfully, "is to have him make a raise, using his expectations as collateral."

This was suggested to Dolly, and the idea pleased him hugely. He was tired of being hard up, and, besides, for nearly a month he had not heard himself termed a perfect gentleman, nor had there been such a tidal wave of enthusiasm for him along Broadway as there had been during the period in which he was making his reputation as a dispenser of hospitality. He was perfectly willing, so he told Mr. Freelance, to give a large bonus to any one who would accommodate him with a loan of ten thousand dollars. The will could be seen at the surrogate's office, and the property, consisting of the house in Madison Square in which he had been born, and certain other parcels of real estate which the prudent Dillenbeck had purchased in his wife's name, was all free and clear of encumbrance, and continually increasing in value. For once in his life Dolly showed a gleam of common sense and placed the matter in the hands of Joe Whitcomb, who was a clear-headed, hard-working, and honest young business man—one who proved himself such by instantly advising his old friend not to break into his inheritance for any such uncertain venture as a theatrical company.

But when Dolly showed him that he had determined to have his way, Joe reluctantly consented to go about among his friends and make as good a bargain for him as he possibly could.

Meanwhile the horizon seemed so dark and uncertain to Mr. Freelance that more than once he expressed to Miss Wheatleigh his intention of throwing up his engagement as manager and returning to his old trade of writing for the newspapers. Then it was Maude who came to the front in a most unexpected and reassuring manner, by confessing that ever since her introduction to the theatrical profession she had been in the habit of putting away small and large sums of money from time to time, so as to be prepared for any emergency.

It will be remembered that Becky Sharp displayed the same kind of prudence and a like reserve concerning it. Poor Becky! There is just one point in her career in which she fairly wins the sympathy of her sex, and that is when her husband compels her to open the little box which contains her treasures.

"Now, not a word of this to Dolly,"

was her condition as she placed a thousand dollars in her manager's hands. "No, I don't want any receipt, for I can trust you. Sometimes I wish that we could get my husband out of the partnership and run the business ourselves— you and I."

"I have been in the theatrical business a dozen years, and this is the first time I ever heard of a woman in it wishing to leave her husband and take up with her manager," rejoined Mr. Freelance, with perfect gravity.

With the little money that Miss Wheatleigh could supply, supplemented by his own business ability, good taste, and financial experience, Mr. Freelance continued, with hopeful mien and anxious heart, the preparations for the first annual tour of the Maude Wheatleigh combination. Paragraphs laudatory of the genius and beauty of his star glistened in the columns of the daily papers. Descriptions of her happy childhood hours along the gem-encrusted beach and among the luxuriant tropical foliage of San Domingo cast their magic spell over newspaper readers of both sexes and of every age. (San Domingo was chosen as her birthplace because Mr. Freelance said that it had not yet produced a great actress and was therefore about due.) Even the "dainty apartment with its choice bric-à-brac and rare etchings" that had done such good service in behalf of Pearl Livingstone was once more brought into requisition; but this time it was graced with a samovar, in order, as Mr. Freelance expressed it, to "bring it up to date and go Livingstone one better."

Very little was seen of Dolly Dillenbeck in these days, for he was not the sort of man to face importuning creditors when it was possible to slip out of sight; and as every day brought its new troubles, Dolly was willing to leave all responsibility on the shoulders of his manager, and devote himself to the task of avoiding everybody. About the middle of September the *High Roller* ceased publication, amid the wails and lamentations of those who held claims against it for goods or services rendered. Dolly had long since ceased to take any interest in the venture, and its collapse did not seem to affect him at all. He was so accustomed to bad luck, he said complainingly, that one blow more or less made no difference to him.

To tell the truth, Dolly's luck in all affairs of chance had been phenomenally bad ever since he first ventured on Broadway. If he played faro he was sure to lose, and if he played poker he generally won during the early part of the evening, but always discovered, when he held a particularly good hand, that somebody else at the table had a better one. He had gambled in Wall Street, speculated in grain, and bought pool-tickets at the races, but always with the same result. The poor fellow had been a marker for blacklegs, adventurers, and rascals of every description ever since he first made his appearance on upper Broadway. In all his career he had not attracted to himself a single true friend except Joe Whitcomb, who was always ready to stand by him, and who had warned him repeatedly against the people with whom he associated.

But it was impossible to make him understand that the gentleman with the fine mustache, piercing eyes, and clear-cut profile, who was so ready to drink champagne with him, and who never failed to declare that he—Dolly—was one of the finest gentleman that the Deity had ever permitted to live on the footstool, could, after such a display of disinterested friendship, deliberately deal to that matchless young Chesterfield three kings and two aces, and to himself four trays and an unimportant card.

He had dropped thousands of dollars in gambling-houses without ever even learning of the existence of what is termed a "brace-box," and he had wagered unheard-of sums at Brighton under the delusion that it was customary for the best horse to win. The horses did not start at Guttenberg until after he had made his bets.

There are some men who are constitutionally incapable of distinguishing between sincerity and that form of deceit which finds its best aid in flattery. Such men are always at the mercy of unprincipled sharps, and will never accept without suspicion the advice of those who are capable and honest enough to be of use to them.

Dolly was a man of this description.

The only paying investment that he had made during his whole career of silly extravagance was the money advanced to Hustle & Hardup for a third interest in the Maude Wheatleigh company. To be sure, he had spent a great deal of money in securing for himself a personal lien on the young lady; but the interest which he held in her professional prospects was one that was well worth the money he had advanced for it, and promised to become still more valuable in the years to come.

One evening Mr. Joe Whitcomb encountered Mr. Freelance in the lobby of an uptown theater, and straightway drew him aside, with a look of importance on his face.

"I was just hoping that I'd run across you somewhere," said Joe, "for this matter of Dillenbeck's has taken a new and surprising turn. Did you ever hear anything about Miss Wheatleigh's childhood?"

"No," replied the manager, carelessly.

"She was born somewhere up in Massachusetts, and I think she told me she worked in a dressmaker's shop, or something of that sort, before she came to New York. Why?"

"Yes, that's it," said the other; "it was in a dressmaker's shop that her husband first saw her. She comes from the same part of the country that he and I do, and I was dead gone on her myself when I was eighteen years old. You never knew that, I suppose?"

Mr. Freelance uttered an exclamation of astonishment. "I cannot understand what reason she had for hiding this from me," he said, thoughtfully.

"What I want to know now," continued Joe, with great earnestness, "is whether she is legally married to Dillenbeck or not."

"There is no doubt of that," said the other, positively. "She's married to him hard and fast."

"That's a very unfortunate thing," said Whitcomb as he sadly shook his head. "Now I understand why the Board of Madagascar Missions is going to contest his mother's will. There is a clause in it, or rather a codicil added a short time before her death, which provides that all the real estate is to go to the Board of Missions in case her son contracts a marriage with Mary Hunt, at that time a resident of Maplefield, Mass. And that Mary Hunt, who was always known as Polly Hunt, is none other than Maude Wheatleigh, now Mrs. T. Adolphus Dillenbeck."

"Well, of all infernal streaks of hard luck, this is the worst that I ever heard of," exclaimed Mr. Freelance, as he sat down on a bench and wiped the perspiration from his brow.

"You see," explained Joe, "the old lady had an idea that Polly wanted to marry her son; and she got so worried about it that she put that codicil in her will so as to prevent it. Well, it's pie for the Madagascar people."

"Yes, and hell for us," said Mr. Freelance, reverently.

## CHAPTER XXII

THERE came a day about the middle of October—a cheery day of blended haze and sunshine, one of the sort calculated to make glad the heart of any one whose business depended on fair weather. On this day Mr. Freelance arose at the early hour of eight, opened the shutters of his bedroom, and looked anxiously up at the serene, cloudless sky. "Thank Heaven for the good weather! That's one of the first pieces of good luck that has come to us in a long while," he said to himself; and then added, with a sigh, "In fifteen hours the curtain will be down and the long agony over. Then I'll be able to form some idea as to whether I've made a fool of myself again, or struck a good thing at last."

Then his thoughts turned to Dolly, and a great and sincere pity took possession of his heart. Since the crushing revelation in regard to the special clause in his mother's will that unfortunate young man had simply "gone all to pieces," as Whitcomb put it, with a rapidity that had shocked even those who had been aware of his true mental condition; and now that the day to which he had been looking forward for so many months, and with such an intense longing, had dawned at last, Adolphus Dillenbeck, but yesterday one of the gayest figures in the town, could have no part in the joys and splendor of Maude Wheatleigh's New York début. He had gone to the White Mountains for his health, was the way in which Maude and Freelance accounted for his long absence from Broadway; and there were but two or three besides them who knew that the White Mountains was a large and gloomy mansion situated in the midst of pleasant gardens, and filled with guests, some silent and sad, others raging like wild beasts, others, again, with smiling, vacant faces, playing contentedly with toys, and all under the watchful eyes of alert, sinewy attendants.

I know that I am missing a great opportunity in not presenting to my readers a graphic picture of the closing hours of poor Dolly Dillenbeck's career. In the hands of a realist—meaning one with a taste for dirt and delirium tremens—the subject might well become the excuse for a revolting study of mental decay in all its repellent phases; but to me the theme is so distasteful,—infinitely more so than death,—so pregnant of sad memories and sadder forebodings, that I have not the heart to probe into it too deeply. I have seen too many old comrades drop out of the ranks and go staggering down the long easy grade until the heavy doors closed upon them and mercifully hid them from view. Let us think of poor George Gaunt, of Bavaria's mad king, of Tittlebat Titmouse, and imagine what this poor simple good-natured spendthrift has become since his mind gave way.

I last saw him entering the St. Anthony café, where there was an unpaid score of colossal dimensions recorded against him. I watched him as he seated himself in an easy-chair, took from his pocket a five-dollar bill, and placed it on the table before him. The man who put out the gas the last time that Edwin Forrest played was seated in a remote corner of the room, and looked on indifferently as Dolly entered and dropped wearily into the leather-covered arm-chair.

"There's a fellow," he remarked to the man with whom he was drinking, "who hain't got a dollar to his name, and can't get a drink in this house unless he shows the price of it first. What's more, he looks to me as if he was a-gittin' a little nutty. I can remember the time when he was a perfect gentleman."

At this moment he caught sight of the five-dollar bill, and, with a hasty adieu to his friend, he darted across the room and seized Dolly warmly by the hand. The bottle of champagne that they drank on this occasion was the last one purchased by the ruined young man, whose swift career is still fresh in the memory of the frequenters of the cafés and theaters on upper Broadway. Dolly's guest saved the cork and tinfoil, and has since made them the basis of a new claim to metropolitan renown. Indeed, his fame as the extinguisher of the gas on Forrest's last night has grown dim since then in the face of the fierce white light that now marks him wherever he goes as the man who drank half of the last bottle of wine that Dolly Dillenbeck opened on Broadway. Moreover, the same bright glare completely effaced the feeble flame of a new and rival celebrity who was beginning at that time to establish a lucrative connection in a number of first-class cafés on the strength of the fact that he had been on the gate the first time that Lydia Thompson appeared in America.

At ten o'clock Mr. Freelance, still thinking pitifully of Dolly, crossed Broadway, and ran almost into the arms of General Whiffletree and Judge Doonothing, who were standing on the curb. It was seldom indeed that those distinguished gentlemen appeared in public at such an early hour, and now there was a haggard look of unrest on the faces of both that told of sleepless nights and long, anxious vigils.

"Is it true that young Dillenbeck has got back to town?" they both demanded, eagerly.

"Certainly," replied Mr. Freelance, with cheerful mendacity. "And he's as bright as a new fiddle—looks as he used to, and feels as well as he looks. He's come back so as to attend Miss Wheatleigh's first performance at the Jollity Theater to-night, and he'll expect to see both of you gentlemen there."

"I shall be very glad to see him," replied the Judge, pompously. "I consider that that young man has treated me in a very shabby and contemptible manner. I've always taken a warm interest in him, and when he started the *High Roller* I devoted a great deal of very valuable time to putting the paper on its feet. I was at his office every day of my life, and attended to a great many important transactions for him without ever asking for a cent in the way of salary. Then at his special request I consented to contribute a few reminiscences—matter, sir, that has never appeared in print before, and proved of incalculable value in booming his miserable journal. I have never been paid for the last of those contributions, sir, and, what's more, sir, Mr. Dillenbeck has not had the decency to answer a single one of the letters that I have written him on the subject. I would like my honorarium for my articles, sir, and, what's more, I propose to have it."

The Judge looked very fierce as he uttered these words, and an expression of sympathy came into Mr. Freelance's face as he regarded him. Then General Whiffletree broke in: "As you know, I had a slight misunderstanding with Mr. Dillenbeck some weeks ago, and for a long while we did not speak to one another. One day, however, we met, and he accosted me in such a friendly manner, and expressed such sincere regret for what had happened, that I believed his repentance genuine, and consented, somewhat against my will, to contribute to his journal. Now, sir, my time is fully occupied with business of far greater importance than writing for the press, but of course I have had a wide experience and have met a great many prominent men in my time, and so, just to oblige this young man, to whom I have stood in the light of a father since he first struck the town, I sat down and prepared some reminiscences of Willard's Hotel, in Washington, and the men who have frequented it during the past twenty-five years. Would you believe it, sir, that young man had the audacity to stop printing his rascally paper on the very day that I sent him my contribution, and I have reason to believe that he did it on purpose to insult me! I consider that he owes me not only the sum of one hundred dollars, the price of my contribution, but also an apology for the manner in which he has treated me. I have heard it stated recently that he has gone wrong in his head and has all sorts of strange delusions. That may account for his behavior in this instance."

"It *is* true that he has delusions," said Freelance, confidentially, as he drew the two genials closer together and addressed them in a low, earnest voice. "Why, he has an idea, General, that he has been lending you money for the past two or three years; and, would you believe it, Judge, he thinks that you got him to cash a draft that you held on somebody in Arkansas, and that the draft came back unpaid. It is curious what fancies take possession of men once in a while," he continued thoughtfully; then, glancing at his watch, he hastily bade them good-morning and darted off before either one of them could recover from his astonishment.

Mr. Freelance found Maude nervously awaiting him. She was pale, fretful and anxious, and burst into tears when he told her that it would be impossible for him to take her to dinner that night, as he had an engagement to dine out.

"I don't see why you should neglect me to-night of all nights in the year," she said as she wiped her eyes. "Where are you going?"

"Now, my dear," said the manager, soothingly, "don't get excited and injure your chances of success. Go out and take a long walk in the park, and try to forget yourself until to-night. I'll see you before you go on, though I shall have my hands full in front. You've only got one thing to worry you, and I've got a hundred. I met an aunt of mine in the street the other day, and she asked me to dine with her to-night and take her to the theater. She wants to see you, and if she likes you she'll talk about you to all the women in town."

Maude took her manager's advice, and thus prepared herself in the best possible manner for the fatigue and excitement of the evening. In the mean time, Freelance, who had been just a little pained to notice that she did not even once refer to Dolly, busied himself with preparations for the night's performance. In the course of the day he soothed the orchestra leader, who was clamoring for his money, calmed a suspicious costumer, and uttered words of hope and encouragement to all whom he encountered about the theater. Then he went home to take a brief nap and dress for dinner.

The aunt with whom he was to dine was a younger sister of his mother, and was scarcely half a dozen years older than himself. She was just entering upon one of the most charming periods of womanhood — that of the half-mourning which succeeds the widow's weeds. He had met her by accident in the street, and she had reminded him of the fact that he had not been to see her for several months, and that Miss Kitty Ingraham, who had long desired to meet him, was spending a few days with her.

"It's all right going to see Aunt Maria and the kids," said Mr. Freelance to himself as he tied his white cravat, "but it's apt to be a bore talking to the girls she has around her."

## CHAPTER XXIII

It was not quite six o'clock when Mr. Freelance rang the bell at Mrs. Esmonde's door and stood for a minute on the threshold, looking out at the quiet street, on which the shadows of a chill autumn evening had already fallen. It was a cheerless outlook — one that seemed to be in complete accord with the dull weight of apprehension and weariness of flesh and soul that hung over his usually buoyant spirits. He had just passed through one of the most trying periods of his whole life, and now that the worst was over, and nothing more serious than the threatened strike of the orchestra or a possible demand from some intractable actor stood between him and either ruin or success, a feeling of numbness and despondency took possession of his senses, and as he stood in the doorway of his aunt's house he felt that he would gladly exchange places with any one who could earn a decent living in some unexciting and commonplace path of life.

Then the door was thrown open, and as he passed into the warm, well-lighted hall, and heard from the regions above an excited shriek of "It's Cousin Billy!" the weight of depression slid from his heart, and all memory of the trouble, the anxiety, the poverty, and the devices to escape it which had been the sum total of his existence for so many months past, vanished from his mind. His careworn face brightened with a smile that Maude Wheatleigh would have given a six months' salary to have won for herself; and then a small child in a short pink dress, and with her long yellow hair streaming out behind her, came flying down the broad staircase and bounded with a joyful cry into his arms.

"Mrs. Esmonde wishes you to go up to the children's nursery, sir," said the servant as he relieved him of his overcoat and umbrella.

"Take me up with you, Cousin Billy," pleaded little Molly. "I want to show you my new doll." Then the manager of the Maude Wheatleigh combination placed little Molly on his shoulders, and together, the child laughing merrily as she clasped him tightly around the neck, they walked up the stairs and presented themselves at the nursery door.

"Come in, William," cried Mrs. Esmonde, who was sitting by the fire with her youngest child on her knee. "Kitty, this is my nephew, Mr. Freelance.—Now, William, you may entertain Miss Ingraham while I tell the children a story. She's dying to know all about your theatrical company and that pretty young woman who's going to appear to-night. I hope you did n't forget to get that box for us."

A remarkably nice-looking young woman acknowledged Mr. Freelance's salutation, leaning forward in her chair and shading her face from the red firelight with a fan of ostrich plumes, while she regarded him through a pair of clear gray eyes.

I have called Kitty Ingraham nice-looking because that is a convenient, non-committal term, which, while it conveys precisely the idea intended, at the same time leaves the important question of beauty to the reader's imagination. To the young man who beheld her now for the first time she seemed singularly beautiful as she sat in a charming, unstudied attitude, with her cheek resting against a mass of soft, trembling plumes. To me, who knew her well, Miss Ingraham was always beautiful—far more lovely, indeed, on the day when I saw her for the last time than she was when we first met. There were some of her friends, however, who maintained that many of her features were faulty, and that if it were not for her eyes, which were wonderfully frank and true, and her smile, which was of irresistible sweetness, she would never be called even pretty.

Surely some folks in this world are very hard to please. A woman engaged in the warfare which engrosses the best efforts of her younger years needs no better equipment than a smile and a pair of eyes like Kitty Ingraham's.

The look which this eminently attractive young woman now bent upon the slim, good-looking young man who stood before her clad in the conventional evening dress which so well becomes a gentleman, and with little Molly still perched upon his shoulders, was one of keen scrutiny; and a certain expression crept into her face which a close observer might have taken as an indication that Mrs. Esmonde's cousin found favor in her sight.

"Yes, Mr. Freelance," she said, leaning back again in her chair, "tell us all about this wonderful young actress whom we are to see to-night. What is she like off the stage? I've seen her photographs, and they're lovely."

Something that might have been a sigh of weariness escaped the visitor's lips. From the moment in which he saw little Molly flying down the staircase he had forgotten the Jollity Theater, the actress who was to play there that night, the orchestra which had threatened not to, the salaries which were long overdue; in short, the child with the streaming curls had driven the "shop" completely out of his mind, and diverted his thoughts to such welcome, refreshing, and uplifting subjects as the new doll, the little gray kitten, and the gold pin with the tiny diamond in it, which was to be worn only on Sundays.

Mr. Freelance must have shown in his face his abhorrence of the whole question of Miss Wheatleigh and her New York début, for Mrs. Esmonde instantly chimed in with: "No, don't tell us anything about her. We'll see her to-night, and then we'll tell you what we think of her. Besides, you must be bored to death with her."

"To tell the truth," said the young man, gratefully, as he dropped into a soft arm-chair before the fire, "I'm glad enough to forget the theater whenever I can, and this is one of the first chances I've enjoyed in a great many weeks."

Miss Ingraham, watching him narrowly, saw the haggard look of unrest that came into his face at mention of the actress's name, and said to herself, "Very likely he's interested in the girl." And then an undefined, inexplicable feeling of resentment toward this pretty young woman with the baby-blue eyes and the graceful figure came upon her unawares and had found foothold in her heart before she knew it. Of course she dislodged the intruder at once, but the irritation that remained for some time afterward was like that which follows the sting of a poisonous insect.

Kitty Ingraham was a girl of a type that is by no means uncommon in New York now, and is, I am glad to say, appreciated at its true worth by those who are fortunate enough to become familiar with it. There were not many girls of her class in the town a quarter of a century ago, and those that did exist here then were looked upon as "queer" or else "advanced," which was considered worse than queer. Her natural taste for the artistic side of life was very pronounced, and had been developed by indiscriminate reading and intimate association with some extremely clever girls. By the way, what a difference there is in point of brains and quickness of perception between the young women who adorn New York society and the men with whom they associate!

Miss Ingraham, although occupied to a great extent with social duties, nevertheless contrived to keep pace with contemporaneous art and letters, and there was nothing that gave her greater pleasure than to make the acquaintance of men and women who were connected in some way with artistic affairs.

Under better conditions than those which exist in the social circles to which she belonged she would have been able to gratify one of her pet ambitions and become an acknowledged leader in those fashionably artistic, literary, and intellectual circles of which she was wont to dream in her waking hours, and which she firmly believed could be gathered together in New York. That is to say, she believed that the separate particles constituting such circles were held in solution in the rest of the body politic, and needed only the hand of some skilled social alchemist to precipitate and gather them up into a compact mass.

In short, she longed to collect about her the ingredients which constitute a "salon"; and in her pet reveries she saw herself moving with the grace and command of a queen among poets, musicians, painters, actors and actresses, honored by them all, the acknowledged center of all that there is of the best in letters and the arts.

Miss Ingraham was not the first woman who has dreamed of transplanting from Paris to New York the French salon, an institution which would thrive in our artistic climate about as well as a pineapple would in Tompkins Square. The mere fact that the mistresses of the Paris salons are able to fill their parlors with celebrities and keep them there for an entire evening without giving them anything to drink shows that our own intellectual and artistic society is far more exacting in its demands than that of the French capital.

Some social historian of New York will one day tell the story of the different attempts that have been made from time to time by clever and ambitious women to establish here a salon on the same plan as those maintained in Paris by Mme. de Staël, Mme. Adam, and their kind. These schemes have always failed, for some reason or other—generally because the women who projected them were either dazzled by the glare of fashion, or else incapable of distinguishing between true fame and mere newspaper notoriety. The quality of the liquor served in many of these salons has in more than one instance been such as to create distrust of the hostess in some of the brightest minds of the day.

As a general thing the New York De Staël has allowed her drawing-rooms to become choked and cluttered up with the people who hang about the skirts of conventional society—those who are occasionally seen at the very large entertainments of the rich and socially influential; on the strength of which distinction they talk continually about their "society friends," and mention them by their given names.

Kitty Ingraham, although one of the very cleverest girls I have ever known, and one, moreover, who had been too well born and reared to be fooled by false social pretensions, nevertheless went completely astray in her estimate of literary and artistic worth, because she found it impossible to divest her mind of the idea that it had some sort of dependence on or connection with "very nice people."

Nice people! I wonder how many of them ever crossed the path of François Villon, except the priest whom he robbed! The road to hell is paved with good intentions, and the road to artistic hell is lined four deep on either side with the very nicest sort of nice people.

Miss Ingraham possessed, among other notably attractive qualities, one that would have been of the greatest service to her had she ever established the salon that occupied such a large place in her waking dreams. She had a genuine interest in art and letters, an interest that showed itself instantly in the brightening of her eyes and the lighting of her whole face whenever she met a writer, an artist, or an actor.

It was this look of eager interest, rendered doubly charming because it was combined with one of approval, that made such an agreeable impression on Mr. Freelance. It was a look that seemed to say to him, "I am glad to see you, because there are lots of things that I would like to ask you regarding the stage and its people. It must be fascinating to know so many actors and actresses, and, besides, I find you decidedly good-looking."

"Cousin Billy" was compelled to tell the children a story before they would permit him to leave the nursery; and Kitty, leaning back in the luxurious depths of her arm-chair and shading her face from the firelight with her big fan, watched the young man narrowly as he set about a task that was by no means irksome to him. Mr. Freelance was an excellent nursery *raconteur*, and he found new favor in the young girl's eyes as he held the youngsters spellbound with some clever flight of fancy.

"He does n't look as if he could care much for that creature at the theater. How could he, when he is so fond of little children?" she said to herself as she watched him. She had made up her mind that Maude was a "creature," which is only another word for "hussy," the term by which Mrs. Dillenbeck had characterized her years before.

A glow of satisfaction warmed the young man's heart as he seated himself at the well-ordered dinner-table, with his aunt and her agreeable young guest on either side of him. The cloth was spotless, the glass and silver had been polished to the last degree, and the servant performed his duties deftly and without noise.

Only a man who has been hard up knows what a relief it is to spend an occasional evening with wealthy people —not for the material benefit that is to be derived from them, but because while in their society he will not be continually reminded of his own poverty. After the terribly depressing struggle through which the young manager had passed, the atmosphere of Mrs. Esmonde's dining-room was a positive balm to his feelings, and he resolved that in the future he would cultivate his aunt's friendship much more assiduously than he had in the past. It was delightful to know that so long as he remained at that table he would hear nothing about how much something had cost, or how much money some perfect gentleman had "blown in" in the course of a single evening, or how many dollars' worth of diamonds had been employed in the bedizenment of some pretentious, underbred woman. It was even a relief to him to observe that Mrs. Esmonde wore very little jewelry and Miss Ingraham none at all, although both women were richly and beautifully dressed.

If I may be permitted to pause here and offer a word of counsel to the ambitious but impecunious young man who stands on the threshold of life, as the

Sunday-school books say, it would be to keep on good terms, if possible, with a few millionaires. So long as you do not try to borrow money from them or to marry their daughters you will find them, on the whole, easy-going and well-disposed folk, who will never say or do anything intended to remind you of the cruel fact that your pockets are empty. In other circles of society the torn coat, the worn-out shoe, the frayed linen, and other familiar indices of poverty are liable to awaken comment, if not actual ridicule. At the same time it must be said that the scoffers are often capable of lending you money with which to renew your wardrobe. In the society of the wealthy, however, your clothes will attract but little attention, because successful men have other ways of judging both purse and character. But do not be tempted by this polite consideration to try to borrow money from, or to make love to the daughters of, these millionaires. It is true that once in a long while a daughter of Mammon is permitted to marry an impecunious young man, but my experience teaches me that millionaires never lend any money except to one another. From this we may gain an idea of their sense of relative values, and at the same time understand why it is that they remain plutocrats even when bereft of their children. In common with the rest of humanity they possess an insatiable thirst for free theater tickets, and are always glad to win the esteem and confidence of those who are in a position to secure them.

There are not many situations that are more agreeable than that in which Mr. Freelance found himself at Mrs. Esmonde's table. Of course there are some who will say that if he had been placed at the same table in company with the one woman whom he loved and who loved him, instead of between two women who merely liked him, the situation would have been infinitely more agreeable to him and interesting to the reader. This I emphatically deny. I cannot change the situation, because I am merely relating what happened, and I would not if I could. Not only was it a genuine pleasure to the young man to find himself in the society of two lovely women, neither one of whom wanted an engagement in his company or a puff in a newspaper, but it was also delightful, in a novel way, to speculate vaguely on the possibilities afforded by the sort of liking that he felt instinctively was springing up between himself and Kitty Ingraham.

It has been the fashion in the trade of cynicism to speak sneeringly of woman's friendship for man. Nevertheless it is an affection that possesses many rare charms, not the least of which is that it seldom degenerates into vituperation.

Mrs. Esmonde's guests supplied most of the talk at the dinner-table that night, while their hostess looked on and listened with amusement and pleasure pictured on her face.

"What a responsive, sympathetic girl!" said Freelance to himself.

"What can such a bright, intelligent fellow see to admire in a mere creature like that actress, with her photograph in every shop-window in town?" was the thought that persistently forced itself into Kitty's mind as she listened to the theatrical manager's talk about some of the experiences through which he had passed.

It was after seven when Mr. Freelance rose hurriedly from his chair and started for the theater. "I've had a beautiful time, aunt, and you can't think how I hate to go away," he said, earnestly. "You need n't leave here till eight, for we don't ring up till a quarter past. I'll come into the box after the first act and find out what you think of my star."

"I do wish that William would spend more of his time with such nice girls as Kitty," said Mrs. Esmonde to herself as she watched him, thoughtfully and affectionately, till the door closed behind him.

# CHAPTER XXIV

"I SUPPOSE that's what may truthfully be called fame," remarked Mr. Freelance as he stood in front of the Jollity Theater with his eyes fixed upon the two three-sheet posters representing Maude Wheatleigh in the great scene of her thrilling war drama. "And to-morrow morning every newspaper in the town will tell the story, more or less truthfully, of to-night's happenings. I think it's the rapidity with which a reputation can be made that lures so many people into the theatrical business. If they had to wait for Homer to get his 'Iliad' finished and into print they'd lose all interest in the game."

Little did those easy-going, pleasure-seeking people, who began to stream into the house as soon as the doors were thrown open, dream of the difficulties and obstacles which had been overcome in order that those wide-swinging green baize doors might be thrown back to permit them to enter. Little did they imagine—these men and women whose imaginations had been skilfully fed with the dainty flat, the rare bric-à-brac, the exquisite Worth costumes—that at that very moment a knot of discontented actors were gathered together behind the scenes, seriously discussing the propriety of making a demand, then and there, for their back salaries; that the box-office was fortified like a beleaguered city, and that Mr. Freelance and his able assistant were prepared to guard against any strategic movement on the part of a deputy sheriff or other designing person.

The house had been "papered" with wonderful skill and ingenuity. Mr. Freelance was no believer in the common practice of giving free tickets to theatrical agents, bartenders, and people of the class who swarm up and down Broadway every afternoon. The very presence of such people in a theater, he argued, indicated that the house had been papered; and, besides, the regular "first-nighters," as they are usually termed, were a blasé, discontented lot who always found fault with the play, the star, the company, and chiefly with the manager who admitted them, and did not hesitate to express their opinions loudly in the lobby between the acts, and in the different public resorts of the city the following day.

Mr. Freelance had been at work for a fortnight previous to the opening, distributing tickets in blocks of five, and in some cases of twelve, among different young people of his acquaintance who dwelt in such remote places as Brooklyn, Orange, and Newark. The result was that the seats thus given away in blocks were occupied by "theater-parties" composed of well-dressed young men and bright, pretty girls carrying bouquets, and looking for all the world like members of the highest aristocracy.

The society reporters and critics, some of whom did not appear until the close of the first act, looked about them for the familiar faces which were never missed on a first night, and not seeing them, but in their stead a dozen large parties of young people in festal array, concluded that it was what is termed a "money house," and their respect for Miss Wheatleigh and the play rose accordingly.

To the dozens of professionals and barroom loafers who applied for admittance, Mr. Freelance gave the stereotyped answer, "Sorry to refuse you, dear boy,"—or "dear girl," as the case might be,—"but there's not a seat left, and we've turned money away already. If you want to go in and stand up, you'll have to see

Hardup, and perhaps he'll pass you. I know he has refused everybody so far."

Great was the grumbling and profanity in the lobby in consequence of Mr. Freelance's firmness, and great was the surprise in the cafés and saloons to which these people repaired, when they made known the fact that the whole town had turned out to see that girl of Dolly Dillenbeck's, and that all the old rounders had been "turned down" at the door.

But for the regular critics, the society reporters, and other members of the press, besides a few managers of importance, Mr. Freelance had a ready smile and a cordial hand-shake. He was well known to most of the critics, and very generally liked because of his tact, good nature, and unfailing good breeding. Some of the leading critics were glad to stop to have a few words with him, and to each one of these he made what he called "a special plea for mercy for my unfortunate client,

Miss Maude Wheatleigh, who now stands before the bar of public opinion."

As for Mr. Hustle, he took no part in the ceremonies incident to Maude's New York début, and while his business manager was attending to a thousand necessary details in the lobby and on the stage, he sat, in company with Mr. Hardup, in the back room of a near-by saloon, safe from the intrusion of process-servers, and in constant communication, through a trusted messenger, with Mr. Freelance.

The latter, passing through the manager's box to the region behind the scenes, came suddenly and unexpectedly upon the convention of discontented mummers, and stopped short to address them.

"I want to tell you something, my friends," he said, speaking very calmly, but with a note of determination in his voice which at once arrested their attention. "This is the night that we've all of us been working and waiting for for months. It is the night that will decide whether we are to sink or swim. I know that you're behind on the salary question, but that's not my fault, and it's not Miss Wheatleigh's fault, either. There're five hundred dollars in the box-office now and there's a line that reaches out to the sidewalk. I've got plenty to do in front to-night, as you can imagine; but I shall have my eyes on the stage, and I take my solemn oath that of the money that is to be divided to-morrow not one cent will go to anybody who misses a cue, puts in a line not written by the author, keeps the stage waiting, or gives a performance that is in any way below highwater mark."

Having thus delivered himself, Mr. Freelance proceeded rapidly to the star dressing-room, where he found Maude in a much more nervous condition than she had been on the night of her Albany début.

"How is it in front, Billy?" she asked

anxiously. "I do hope that the orchestra has n't struck yet, and that you fixed that dreadful printer and coaxed the company into going on. You know I 've been so worried and bothered with all this trouble we 've had that I feel more like sitting down on the floor and crying than going out on that stage and acting."

"My dear," replied the other, as he placed his hand gently on her bare white shoulder, "everything is all right, and everybody is satisfied and contented. Stop thinking about your troubles, and simply do your best and look your prettiest. I have as much to do in front as you have on the stage."

Of course all the members of the St. Anthony House brigade had free seats on this important occasion. Mr. Freelance greeted each one with great cordiality, knowing well that they could be depended on for timely and vigorous applause. They inquired, with thirst written all over their faces, how soon Mr. Dillenbeck was expected, and were glad to learn that he could be looked for before the close of the first act.

"He's particularly anxious to see all you gentlemen," said the business manager, suavely, "for I think he's got a little surprise in store for you."

Then he turned away to greet a dramatic critic whom he knew, told the program-boy to keep his eye on a suspicious-looking character who looked as if he might be the emissary of a printer, and promised a hawk-like Hebrew costumer fifty on account the next morning, if he would only "go away and not queer the show by shoving his ugly beak into the box-office every five minutes."

At the close of the second act the house rose with enthusiasm, in which General Whiffletree and the other genials joined with sanguine heartiness, for they still believed that Dolly would be present to pour foaming wine down their parched throats. They were mopping their brows when they came out into the lobby.

"It's a very queer thing," said Freelance, mysteriously, as he gathered them together in a corner, "but Mr. Dillenbeck can't be found anywhere; and it's very unlucky for me, because he made elaborate preparations for entertaining his friends here to-night. You know what sort of a man he is?"

The genials swore with hoarse oaths that of all large-hearted, jovial gentlemen and wine-openers, Dolly Dillenbeck was the king.

"Then," continued Mr. Freelance, "you may readily believe that he intended to surpass himself to-night. He ordered, a week ago, a supper at one of the principal hotels in the town, and never told me what hotel it was. There's that supper waiting now, the wine in the cooler, and the favors lying at each plate."

"Favors!" gasped Dolly's friends in chorus. "What do you mean by that?"

"Why," rejoined Mr. Freelance, looking at the eager, haggard faces before him, "this is his birthday, and he intended to give every one of his guests a little souvenir of the occasion—some little trifle like a gold watch or a diamond scarf-pin—some little thing like that, because he does n't stop at anything in the way of spending money, you know."

"Great God!" cried Mr. Rungdown, hoarsely, "can't the man be found anywhere?"

"We 've hunted everywhere," exclaimed Freelance, earnestly, "and I 'm afraid that he 's sent a message here which has failed to reach us, been lost or mislaid, or something. He 's not at his hotel, he 's not at the St. Anthony House, and he 's not here. I think if you gentlemen were to take a stroll up Broadway as far as Fiftieth Street and downtown to Fourteenth, you 'd find him somewhere. I know the supper is ordered, for I saw him making out the list of wines, and you 'd think from the quantity that he put down that he was going to entertain a regiment."

The genials instantly started on the search, General Whiffletree and Judge Doonothing turning their faces to the north, and the others spreading themselves like a skirmishing party so as to reach all important strategic points to the east, west, and south as quickly as possible. The manager watched them until they were out of sight, and then went up to pay his respects to his aunt and Miss Ingraham in the upper box.

"I think she's charming, William," exclaimed Mrs. Esmonde, enthusiastically, as her nephew dropped into a chair by her side.

"And what do *you* think of my star?" he said to Miss Ingraham.

"I think she is very clever and very

pretty indeed," she replied, turning upon him a searching look from the depths of her clear, truthful gray eyes. "At any rate, she looks as if she were a wonderfully sympathetic woman. Do tell me how many men have fallen in love with her, and whether she has fallen in love with anybody herself."

"There's one man," replied Freelance, "who was sufficiently in love with her to put her on the stage, spend a lot of money on her, and finally marry her, all of which is a good deal for a man to do for one woman."

Kitty Ingraham was ashamed of the sudden sense of relief and exaltation which the young man's words gave to her, and all at once she found herself feeling much more cordially toward Miss Wheatleigh, who was, she admitted, an extremely brilliant and beautiful woman, and was undoubtedly a good wife to the man who had done so much for her.

"I just seen a couple of deputies go round to the stage door," said the program-boy, in a low whisper, as he drew Mr. Freelance out of the box; and then the manager excused himself to the ladies and disappeared, the curtain went up, and Miss Ingraham found herself enjoying the third act far more thoroughly than she had the previous ones.

Maude Wheatleigh's success that night was a repetition, on a larger scale, and on a much surer footing, of that which she achieved in Albany the year before. Her great scene in the third act raised her audience to a tremendous pitch of enthusiasm, which did not need the exertions of Whiffletree and the rest to make it effective. It was after this act that one of the shrewdest managers in the country strolled carelessly up to Mr. Freelance in the lobby, and said, in a low tone, "Has Hustle got a cast-iron, copper-riveted contract with that woman?"

And Mr. Freelance, knowing well the full import of his words, and all that they signified, coming as they did from him, replied, "I should rather think he had; I helped to draw it up myself."

And then two or three critics came out, putting on their overcoats, on the way downtown to finish their night's work; and one of these stopped and said, "Billy, I think that woman will catch the town."

Mr. Freelance stood in the lobby, smiling affably upon the people as they streamed out of the theater. He always made it a practice on first nights to stand by the gate and look confident and happy, no matter what his private feelings might be.

Mrs. Esmonde and Miss Ingraham stopped to speak to him, and he went with them to their carriage.

"Come home with us and have some supper," said his aunt. But he shook his head. He had a great deal to do, he said, before he could leave the theater. He would call soon, though, for he had not had such a pleasant dinner for a long time. He was sorry he had promised to — to — attend to some matters of business that night, for he would be delighted to have some supper with them and learn exactly what they thought of the whole performance — star, play, and all — in detail. The only opinions that were worth anything, he thought, were those of people who belonged to the paying public. An actor's views were worthless. And then he hastily bade them good-night, told the coachman "home," and returned to his place in the lobby.

Maude Wheatleigh was waiting for him, dressed, and with her cloak lying on the trunk beside her, when he tapped at her dressing-room door. She was nervous and excited, and her eyes sparkled as she greeted him.

"You've been more than any one to me,

Billy," she said wistfully, as she pressed his hand between her two gloved ones.

"We'd better go right along if you're ready," he remarked carelessly.

As they stood at the corner of Broadway waiting for the cable-car, Senator Hardscrabble loomed up out of the autumn mists, and said in dry, hopeless accents, "Have n't seen anything of that party yet, have you?"

"Not yet," replied the manager, gravely. "I'm beginning to get anxious about him."

Maude chattered incessantly on the way home, but her companion paid scant attention to what she said. Kitty Ingraham, with her high-bred face, her exquisite smile, and her honest gray eyes, and poor demented Dolly Dillenbeck were in his thoughts now, and would not be driven out. Maude wondered with suspicious fear why he was so absent-minded.

"Come in and have some supper," she

said persuasively, as they stood on the steps of the apartment-house in which she had taken rooms when she left the expensive hotel to which Dolly had taken her after their marriage.

"No, I think I'll go home; I'm very tired," replied Freelance, with a note of hesitation and uncertainty in his voice that did not escape her keen attention.

"Then good-night. I'm sorry you won't stop," she said, holding out her hand.

But instead of taking it he stood irresolutely on the step below her, looking far up the street, and apparently weighing possibilities and probabilities in his mind.

"Good-night," she repeated, speaking with infinite gentleness and tenderness.

But he still stood there, irresolute, uncertain of himself.

THE END.